Around the
Baobab Tree

A Christian missionary nurse
recounts her experience in Africa

PART II

E. Charlese Spencer

(miss) E. Charlese Spencer, om
RN, scm, mn
CEd, S/L

4, 2006

Around the Baobab Tree:
A Christian missionary nurse recounts her experience in Africa
Part II

Published by Iceni Books™.
610 East Delano Street, Suite 104, Tucson, Arizona 85705, U.S.A.
www.icenibooks.com

ISBN: 1-58736-554-5
LCCN: 2005910448

I lovingly dedicate *Around the Baobab Tree* to the remainder of my nieces and nephews. I missed their formative years while I was being auntie to other peoples' children in Africa, Europe, and America for over 25 years. They are: James Michael, David Edward II, Roxanne Marie, Darrin Lee, Darrald Ray, Vicki Lynn, Kurt Bradley, and *another Roxanne*. My heart's desire and prayer to God is that they will make God's plan for their lives a major priority, down to the smallest detail.

ACKNOWLEDGEMENTS

F OR PERUSAL OF CHAPTERS, from the beginning to the end, I am grateful to Ann Fisher, my co-worker for most of those years, Calvin and Yvonne Spencer, R. Kenneth George and his secretary, Linda Canales, and finally, to my late cousin Linda Bratcher Crider, who will never read the finished product. The picture of the baobab tree on the front cover of the book was provided by Henry Garlock, the man at the base of the tree. He is the mission official who first sent me out to Africa.

TABLE OF CONTENTS

PREFACE

July 1996 Albuquerque, New Mexico: Rev. and Mrs. Paul W. Savage, NMDC 1981-1993.

WE HAVE KNOWN CHARLESE (Spencer) for many years, even before she started her nurses training. We kept up with her progress, her call to missions, and her ministries of mercy in Ghana. We were able to be a part of the work by praying and giving for projects under her supervision.

We prayed especially when one of the village girls was to be married to an idolatrous man and for the daring rescue that Charlese engaged in, nearly costing her life. She lives with injuries that are now a daily reminder of the heroic act.

Charlese has been a faithful servant in whatever capacity she is called upon to fulfill in the NM District and has represented us well. Her personal life is above reproach. We are glad for the writing of her book and look forward to reading it.

—Paul and Ruth Savage

Paul Savage departed this life September 2003; Ruth lives in Texas.

FOREWORD

February 1997 Springfield, MO: Rev. and Mrs. Raymond H. Hudson NMDC Superintendent 1955-1968.

SOME OF THE TIMES and incidents you wrote about brought memories we had almost forgotten. You must have had hours of pleasure as you made this effort to remember and record the stories of your life as a missionary in Ghana. Sister Charlese, you did a great and lasting work in Africa. It was a great pleasure for me, while serving as General Treasure of the General Council of the Assemblies of God, to have brethren from Ghana come into my office to greet me. They told me they were brought to Christ, trained, or influenced in some way by you. Most were serving as officials of the Ghana Assemblies of God at the time. You won many and saw many churches built. Your reward will be great. Keep looking up and ahead. The best is before us. His Coming! It may be soon.

—Raymond H. and Onie Marie Hudson

CHAPTER ONE

Back to the Konkombas, 1969
Changes in Ghana

WHILE TEACHING NURSING IN Wichita, Kansas in the summer of 1967, I received re-appointment to Ghana, West Africa as a missionary-nurse. In March 1968, I moved from Kansas back to my home state of New Mexico with three goals in mind: to itinerate, look for a co-worker, and return to Africa *ASAP*! Gladys Newbill wrote from Mission Headquarters. She was to send me the names of nurses even remotely interested in Africa. One was Joy King in New York. A postscript said Joy King and Sharon Wallace were interested as a team. (They wrote me, asking for slides to help them itinerate. When they returned the slides, they said they would go for midwifery in Great Britain before going to Ghana. Hopefully, my co-worker and I would be in Ghana to welcome them!) The name that interested me most was Ann Fisher, because she lived in Lubbock, Texas, near New Mexico! I wrote Ann and we set a date to meet in March. Betty Olsen was traveling with me as planned to help in my itinerary. We drove to that appointment in Lubbock and met Ann Fisher in her parents' home for only one hour before Ann had to go to work. Among other things, that said Ann was faithful to her responsibilities! I wrote to Everett Phillips at Mission Headquarters, "I found Ann to be interested, while expressing herself well. I feel she would be an asset to the missionary family. She is an RN, working on a degree, and claims a call of God to missionary nursing. One item disturbs me a bit; I am the age of her father! Before I left, Ann declared, 'I'm anxious to get there.' Her Pastor, Morris Sheets, seemed supportive of her plans. I DID NOT suggest that she be my coworker." Later, Everett Phillips replied, "Inasmuch as her pastor is encouraging her, perhaps they could send her off without too much time. I was thinking in terms of her being a coworker for yourself; knowing you already have the midwifery training."

Our first service to present my current plans for returning to Africa was March 13 at Fort Sumner; Darrel Blakely was pastor. New Mexico Missions Secretary booked us once every night and twice on Sunday up to the annual New Mexico District Council Session in April. Jerry Roberts, State Youth Director, was having Sectional Speed-the-Light rallies daily to raise money for overseas vehicles for us who went; we were to attend when near.

At First Assembly in Roswell, where Edgar Newby and his wife pastored, the cash and value of medical supplies donated amounted to over one thousand dollars. It seemed that Betty almost wanted me to give it back; she was usually on the giving end. While the money was not for her, she was included in their enthusiastic welcome. Someone suggested she might go to Africa with me, but she was not a nurse. After a service at Central Assembly in Roswell, we went over the mountain to Alamogordo, where Tommy and Linda Crider pastored with their young children, Davona and Daron.

By March 20, we were in TorC, New Mexico with my parents. I presented my mission plan to Pastor and Mrs. Harold Hill and First Assembly. The next day, my parents took Betty and me up the Monticello Creek to their ranch.

As we started our return trip, we had a flat tire. We drove toward Winston and the Black Range Mountains to a gas station. While the tire was being repaired, we saw a "Café" sign in a window. We went in and ordered blue cornmeal enchiladas. They were topped with an egg, sunny-side up! Betty said she never before put blue food in her mouth and the soft cooked egg on top made it difficult. She has told me JUST HOW DIFFICULT many times! After she learned to eat it, I gave her blue cornmeal for Christmas one year.

From TorC, we went to Albuquerque to have seven services in and around the city in seven days. Our first was with Pastor Everett Smith and family, at Valley Gospel Tabernacle. His sister, Grace Thomas, and family had gone to the Gold Coast of Africa even before I did. When I spoke at Revival Tabernacle, I told Pastors F.W. and Mary Watkins that I had met friends and family of theirs in Kansas. At mid-week, we were at Albuquerque's West Mesa Assembly. I had my very first presentation ever in 1953 at that church! The same pastors, Wesley and Charlotte (Johnson) Smith, and family were still there in 1968. At the time of writing and the printing of this book, in the 2000s, Charlotte Johnson-Smith's mother, Edna Johnson, age 90s, supports me monthly. She and others who supported my efforts in Africa started supporting me again when I went into a motorized wheelchair because of painful Arachanoiditis (chronic, sterile, meningitis with no treatment, no cure, and listed under research supported by the Jerry Lewis' telethon.) First Assemblies in Alamogordo, Albuquerque, and Carlsbad, in New Mexico continue with financial help! The same is true of an individual in Texas and one in Alaska. I understand when support must drop off to meet current needs in someone's life or church! I consider it a miracle that some continue. Attorney William J. Lock and his wife, Judy, have helped with investments and legal advice for retirement.

Meanwhile, *back at the ranch!* We managed to be in Estancia with Pastor Forrest Mason, in Los Lunas, where Pastor J.A.

Deweber and family pastored for years and in Mountainair where Pastors Paul and Lena Harrington were pastoring and semi-retired. (I packed in their garage in Albuquerque for my first trip to Africa in 1953.) Then we drove to Gallup where I had first met Betty and her sister, Anna. The Adrian Harper family was still pastoring as before. We had a service with them and at two Indian churches. They seemed to enjoy seeing slides of the Ghanaian churches, pastors, Bible schools, and students.

When it was time for New Mexico District Council in Las Cruces, we parted. Betty Olsen went from Gallup back to Kansas, got her stored belongings, and moved to Denver where her brother was located. After I went back to Africa, she sometimes drove from Colorado to Truth or Consequences, New Mexico to be with my parents for holidays. Her parents, immigrants from Norway, were both deceased. Betty is a proud, first-generation American. Still, you had to remember that she was from Long Island, New York. My parents took her to Juarez Mexico. She left a cafe without eating when she saw the price of the meal in pesos. She said, "Nothing that goes into my mouth is worth that!" My dad explained the money exchange and she did eat.

New Mexico District Council was held the first week in April 1968 at Las Cruces. Marie Hudson, New Mexico Women's President, asked me to speak for the WM's Council breakfast. Raymond Hudson was the Superintendent and State Missions Secretary; Earl Vanzant was Assistant. Thomas Zimmerman, International Superintendent, was speaker. In one particular session of the council, these three men gave me quite a surprise. They said I had traveled enough; I needed to go help Ann Fisher in West Texas, as we were needed in Ghana NOW! In that one service, they raised the rest of my fare, freight, and monthly pledges! Rev. Vanzant said, "She wants to go to Africa; let's *get her out of here!*" He always said that! But, they did not know Ann, my possible co-worker for Saboba. She was a "Hey-Mom-I'd-rather-do-it-myself" person—I liked that!

Just before New Mexico District Council the first week in April 1968, I heard from Morris Sheets, Ann Fisher's pastor. He sent a copy to the New Mexico officials, and it triggered their actions. His letter was positive about Ann. He asked if I could "come to Lubbock to get acquainted with her church and he could announce about Ann's going to the field." I knew he had talked with Everett Phillips when he said my being older than Ann might be an asset because of her youth. A copy of my reply went to Rev. Metzger, West Texas Missions Secretary. I told what happened about my finances at the New Mexico Council. A date was set for me to go to Ann's home church and to West Texas District Council later in April. On the way, I went to Snyder, Texas to visit and have a service at Rev. Vernon and Mrs. (Ozella Reid, a nurse from Ghana clinics) Hager's church. I met their young son, Phillip, for the first time; they had adopted!

I went to Lubbock for the West Texas District Council in April as planned. I met Rev. Rogers, Superintendent and Rev. Metzger, Missions Director for West Texas. I was given the opportunity to explain the clinic crisis to a women's group, although one of their missionary ladies was the main speaker. It seemed Ann was not going to have much trouble getting the required cash for travel and freight. Rev. Thomas Zimmerman, International Superintendent, was speaker in Texas, same as he had been in New Mexico. He asked, "How are plans for a new house in Saboba coming?" I had no good news, as I was being rushed. Ann kept busy with meetings in West Texas; I accompanied her at times, but she did it her way.

Everett Phillips applied for a vehicle for me through Jerry Roberts, New Mexico Youth Director, even before I asked. He never forgot that Helen and I were without a vehicle so long in our first term! At first, he suggested I take over Ruby's blue pickup. It had been driven many miles since Ruby left and even the extra set of new tires Ruby took out had been mounted. I was not too keen on another used vehicle. Edwin Ziemann wrote me from Takoradi with a suggestion about vehicles for Saboba Clinic. He said we needed Ruby's truck, but we also needed a smaller car to save gasoline. He recommended I allow him to get a new Volkswagon with New Mexico's $4,000 Speed-the-Light money. Then Ann Fisher, or whoever came with me, could apply for STL help and transfer Ruby's pickup to her. That sounded good. Just before Ann Fisher and I left America at Christmas 1968, a last-minute cable arrived from Eddie Ziemann in Takoradi. "I ordered your Volkswagen today. Have $2,000 in your STL account immediately. Ruby's truck will be waiting here." We would have transportation when we got to Ghana! Rev. Verne McKinney, in charge of ordering Speed-the-Light (STL) vehicles at headquarters, requested slides for later promotion.

Even before Ann was under appointment, desperate letters kept coming form the Mission Chairman, Bob Cobb, "We are going to lose the clinic in Saboba because it has been closed too long." I knew it was true! However, I had questions.

1) Are nurses going to live with this guilt forever, if we either lock up a clinic or do not get back to one in time?

2) Will we work our bodies into cancer, our hearts into burnout, only to have a committee close the clinic as they did Techimantia?

3) Why must churches become indigenous, but clinics be milked to the end by tired American nurses, only to be closed without medical aid within the borders of a tribe that has been converted to Christ through clinics?"

I felt it was time to get Ghanaian nurses and midwives involved with the mission clinics. Schools, absent at Saboba Clinic's beginning, were now producing potential candidates for higher education. That way, the clinics need not close for lack of American personnel. The Bimoba and Konkomba pastors were becoming strong, as the American nurses were too busy to do area pastoring. We could counsel, support, and have ministers' seminars. Pastors graduating at Kumbungu Bible College were ready for this kind of challenge. Medical clinics work the same. My on-call-24-hours-a-day could not end with tetanus taking its toll on the tiny tots again! I picked brains for ideas. I talked with Joan Wells at Wesley School of Nursing. I talked to Ruby Johnson, a midwife with a Masters. I mentioned *indigenous clinics* in a letter to Everett Phillips and later talked with him at School of Mission time. To my surprise, he said I could, ". . . feel free to think and plan toward *indigenous clinics*, as the Foreign Missions Committee in USA felt it might be the way to go."

He and I wrote to Mission Officials in Ghana about getting Ghanaian nurses and midwives trained to supervise the clinics when Americans were on furlough. Their first reaction was an explosive "No!" as expected. Letters were polka-dotted with words like *insurmountable* and *finances* and *we need you NOW*." It seemed they wanted one warm body in Saboba to "save the ranch!" I wanted at least two warm bodies there to begin with!

What I did find when I got to Ghana was that the government paid fees for training nurses and midwives; we only did things such as buy an extra book, uniform, a watch or gave them money for transportation home on holidays. On graduation, the nurse or midwife would be assigned to our clinics. We would need to pay their salary as long as they worked for the Mission, but low patient fees could cover that.

I went to Kansas the first week in May where I visited Roberta (Bobby) Thiry, partly because she had recently lost her husband. Adriel and Mark were their children. Bobby was still a Wesley School of Nursing employee. I made appointments to speak nearby and attended the Kansas District Council at Central Assembly, my home church while living in Wichita. The Kansas District Council was celebrating its 50th anniversary. Rev. Thomas F. Zimmerman was speaker again; he wailed, "Charlese, are you following me or am I following you?" He knew he was safe in the "council mob!" The Lowenbergs were re-elected as Kansas District Superintendent and Women's Director. Mrs. Lowenberg took me to their ladies' *Sunflower Room*, where I chose a set of stainless steel table service and other items for Africa. They were sent to Houston Harbor to connect with our freight going to Ghana.

I did go to the School of Missions in Springfield, but left three days early to fulfill the promise to Mary Waldon. I spoke for their Women's Day at the Louisiana District Council June 12. Mary helped book me for a later service with another New Mexico transplant, Joy Hoyle from Clovis. She was married to Pastor James Cason in Shreveport. I found Pastor W.W. (Buster) Deerman at Emerson, Arkansas. His parents, Willis and Anne Deerman, were pastors in New Mexico, as was his brother, Steve. In 1953, Helen Kopp and I saw these teenage brothers baptized in the Rio Grande River, before we went to Africa the first time. J.W. and Norma Jean Bobo were pastors at Louisville, Arkansas; I spoke in their church. Norma Jean was a teenager when I worked with her aunt, Grace Davis, in a school bookstore in Waxahachie, Texas. "Mercy," I thought, "I don't remember growing older; when did she?" (Both Grace Davis Embry Smith and Norma Jean Taylor Bobo departed this life before my book was printed.)

In September, I started taking booster and immunizations for going back to Africa; Ann Fisher did also. They were for typhoid, paratyphoid, cholera, polio, diphtheria, and tetanus. Smallpox made me lose my hearing for a few days, as usual. On every furlough, I had keratosis removed by freezing. A dermatologist wrote, "The tumor on the side of your nose is cancer; make an appointment for treatment." My first brush with any cancer! After surgery, they declared the cancer gone; it was found in time. The sun in New Mexico and Africa is death on skin.

Part of October was spent in Lubbock helping Ann, her family, and church any way possible. That was because I planned to drive west, just inside New Mexico, to the Annual Youth Convention in Clovis First Assembly. Melvin Sasse and family pastored there. I also had a service across town at Bethel Assembly with Pastor Victor Elliott and family. It was time to start packing for Africa, so I headed toward TorC by way of Hobbs to bid the Hudsons and my parents farewell. Somehow, I knew the Hudsons were fishing with Marie Hudson's brother, Holly Stewart, and wife, Dorothy. Their children, Doris, David, and Steven, were special to Hudsons and me; they had lost a wee sister to cystic fibrosis. In Hobbs, I received a call from Mom; Dad was critical with lead poisoning. I stopped in El Paso long enough to bid my Uncle Jack, Mom's brother, farewell; he owned apartment houses. He promised to hunt for porta-potties to replace the tin cans in Saboba! In TorC, my dad slowly recovered and left the hospital. While we waited, Mom helped me pack non-perishable items in metal drums with removable lids that locked with rings and a padlock. We opened napkins, facial, and toilet tissue for packing; it would be used later! Now and then, we tossed in packets of silica to keep the contents dry at sea and in Ghana's wet season. Then we poured dry pinto beans into the barrels and shook them to fill every tiny empty space. Woe, if the beans got wet and swelled! I hauled my freight to Compton Anchor Trailer Sales on Route 66 in East Albuquerque. Friends helped complete packing. Frank Powers crated porta-potties and such, as he had done since 1953! In November, Navajo Freight shipped my nine drums and two wooden crates *without* charge to the Houston Long Reach Docks. W.R. Zanes & Company would ship them to Ghana on the Delta Line, *with* charge! That evening I ate with Frank and Louise Powers. Their daughters, Gerelda and Barbara, had married and left the nest.

Ann Fisher flew from Lubbock to New Mexico and I rushed her around to meet church officials, pastors, friends, and my family. Earl Vanzant was now Superintendent of NMDC and his wife, Rowena, was Women's Director. D.B. Chaney was Secretary-Treasurer; his wife was Beunah (Ragland). Jerry Roberts was still Youth and Education Director. Ann and I went out to eat with Karen Hughes, a friend, after a morning service at Central Assembly where the G.B. Mannings were pastoring. In the evening, we went to First Church where the Eugene McClains were pastoring. That church sent me to Africa the first time in 1953, but it had moved from North Second Street to San Pedro, Northeast. Finally, Ann and I drove to TorC where she met my family. Back in Texas, she wrote, "Words could never express what it meant to meet your family and friends. In Africa, I will recall those few days! Merry Christmas!"

The local TorC *Herald* and *Sentinel* newspapers announced:

> A former student of Hot Springs High School and a graduate of UNM, Elsie Charlese Spencer, BSN, SCM (England), is going back to Africa for the third time. She attended Hot Springs schools five years. She was a classmate of both Mrs. Harry Smith and Mrs. Guy Martin, business people in TorC. Assemblies of God churches in New Mexico and West Texas will sponsor the nurses.

I spent the last part of December in Albuquerque having appointments with Dentist Clifford, Orthopedic Surgeon-Rancher Turner (he wore cowboy boots), and Dermatologist Levson. I sold my car. I felt well and ready for three years in Africa. AAA prepared a travel schedule for us. I flew via TWA to Amarillo, Texas on Christmas Day in the snow. I was an overnight houseguest of the E.R. Fosters, parents of Kathleen (Foster) Stafford. Glenn and Kathleen (Kay) Stafford made foreign missions their career also. The day after Christmas, Ann's family drove on snowy roads from Lubbock to Canyon to let Ann say goodbye to her Fisher Grand-parents before coming to Amarillo. The Fishers had migrated to Canyon from California. (My mother was born in Canyon in 1905!) I had said good-bye to my family and friends in Albuquerque, New Mexico the day before. My mind *ran it by again* as I watched Ann bid farewell to her family at the Amarillo Airport.

Whether planned or not, TWA Flight 158 stopped in Wichita *just to exit and board passengers.* My Lowenberg friends from church and Wesley School of Nursing instruc-tors, Helen Halstead and Joan Wells with her little gra'ma, were waiting on the snowy tarmac. When I explained to the stewardess, she allowed me off to greet them. Joan, my former co-instructor, presented me with a copy of the huge *Obstetric Course Outline* that she and I worked so hard to produce. They assured me it was workable; what a farewell gift! That was my last time to see Joan Wells, as both she and Miss Ilse Steg, Wesley School of Nursing Director, died of cancer. The Lowenbergs handed me two farewell cards from Martha Derby at Coldwater and Mrs. H. Erick's at El Dorado, officers in their hometown women's organizations; they would not forget to pray for us. "It is best to go to Africa without people's money than without their prayers!" (Jude 2). "If thy presence go not with me, carry us not up hence." (Exodus 33:15).

At a stopover in Kansas City, I phoned Ruby Johnson at the College of Nursing in Hays. I needed last minute news of Ruby; the Konkombas would ask me! At LaGuardia Air-port in New York, I discovered that one suitcase was already missing. The cover design was *African boutique cloth.* With that one description, TWA located it before we left New York; a tag had come off. We phoned Betty Olsen's sister, Ruth, at Bethpage on Long Island. She had been a guest in my house in Wichita. Ann and I stayed two nights with Ruth, Marie and other Olsen siblings in the three-story family home Betty had described to me. Ruth, being concerned that we had no fur-lined boots, took us to a closet where she fitted us from items left by others coming from Europe and going to places in America where it was not so cold. It snowed the whole two days that Ruth guided us around New York City to places she knew visitors wanted to see; she was an expert! She said, "Take the boots with you; you will need them in England. You will not need them in Africa, so leave them in England where someone can wear them back to us!" We laughed; we thought she was joking!

At Kennedy Airport in New York, we sat waiting longer than expected. The intercom announced that TWA's flight 700 was experiencing technical difficulty; the Boeing 727 was to take us to London. After boarding, we sat again. The pilot said, "Ladies and gentlemen, we still have a leak in this thing; we are chewing bubble gum as fast as we can." I wrote to my brothers in-flight about this, as they worked for Boeing in Seattle. At 9 P.M. on December 28, a snowplow cleared the runway at Kennedy Airport and the *leaky plane* took us safely to London. I was amazed how soon we saw the sun coming up ahead of us; we raced toward it as it came racing toward us.

We got to London at 7:40 A.M. on the 29th and followed the directions in a letter we had from Phyllis Jones. She wrote:

> I'm so excited at the thought of seeing you and meeting your friend, Ann. I'm spending Christmas with the Wallace family. You and Ann come directly to their home in Surrey County. We will go north from there to my house together. Barbara is delighted to have you.

We sped south by rail to Surrey County, past Red Hill, the town where Helen Kopp and I took three months of our midwifery training. (Some say parts of the female side of my Layman ancestors came from Surrey County, England. They also say the Lehmann side from Germany changed their spelling to Layman.) Phyllis Jones met our train at Hazelmere, and took us to the Wallace home at Hazel Grove. Reginald, Barbara, and their daughter, Elizabeth, were home for Christmas. All but Ann had been in Africa; our visit was filled with nostalgia. After our plane ride and all-day visit, Ann and I sped back to London to our reserved hotel room and slept soundly! The next morning, we met Phyllis at London's Kings Cross Station and rode a fast train north to Harrogate. We took a taxi to Silverhill Cottage in Pateley Bridge, where we stayed two days with Phyllis. The rolling hills were green in December and had low rock walls dividing neat plots of land. On the last day of 1968, we toured York by bus and on foot with Phyllis. We desert girls were grateful for Ruth's fur-lined boots; it was damp and cold in England! That night Phyllis heated the covers and put hot bricks to our feet. We spent Wednesday, New Year's Day, traveling to Edinburgh, Scotland, where we checked into a Royal Britisher Hotel. It was cold and we missed the hot bricks! The next morning Ann and I shopped and went to Balmoral Castle. The flag was flying to indicate the Queen was in her northern residence, so we could not enter.

Back at our hotel, Becky Davison joined us from Redcar, a village in Yorkshire near the North Sea. She said her nurse co-worker, Anne Symonds, had not come to greet us because a family member was very ill. North Colchester, where Anne lived, was south toward London and east toward the continent. Becky and Anne would soon be going to Yendi, forty miles from us in Saboba. We mentioned Ruth's boots to Becky. She did not know Ruth Olsen in New York, but told us *exactly where to leave the boots in London* for someone to wear them back to New York!

The three of us ate lunch with Hilda Palenius at the hospital cafeteria where she was taking her midwifery. Of course, we talked about Virginia Turner, a casualty to fatigue from itinerating. She could have been taking her midwifery with Hilda had she survived the auto accident. We talked about Saboba and the Konkombas; all but Ann Fisher had lived there. Becky went home after lunch. Hilda took Ann and me on a tour of the Royal Infirmary where she was studying midwifery and where Sir Alexander Fleming discovered penicillin in 1945. He died ten years later, *hopefully not from bacteria,* while Helen and I were in Saboba. He may not have lived to know what a favor he did for fungus and immune bacteria; they are having a heyday! That evening we attended church with Hilda.

On January 3, Ann and I traveled back south toward London. We stopped for one night with the Daltons in Bedford. Jane, their daughter whom I had delivered, was beautiful. Sheila, Jane's mother, wrote later:

> We were thrilled to bits that you and Ann stayed the night with us. In fourteen years, you have not changed; I would have known you anywhere. Ann made a big hit with Jane.

In London, we stayed two days and three nights at the Ariel Hotel and saw London via the subway tubes. We just *had* to see where David Livingston was buried in Westminster Abby. Repairs to missile-damaged St. Paul's Cathedral had been extensive since Helen Kopp and I first saw it. Fortunately, the Crown Jewels were on display in the Tower of London. The Tower Bridge and Madam Tusaud's Wax Works were worth seeing again. At the tropical supply house, we *looked* at mosquito boots, bought mosquito netting and batteries for my short wave Roberts radio. We would listen to The Voice of America and Billy Graham via Monrovia, Liberia as they waved in and out for another three years. On our last day in London, Reginald Wallace took us to lunch at the British Commonwealth Society in London; Ghana was now a member!

On January 7, 1969, we dropped *Ruth's boots* at the specified address and took a taxi to Heathrow Airport. Flight 707 on Ghana Airways, at 11:30 A.M. Greenwich Mean Time, flew us directly south. We crossed the Mediterranean Sea and an entire north-south swath of the Sahara Desert to land in Accra at 7 p.m. We were still within Greenwich Mean Time east to west, but dropped from fifty degrees latitude to five degrees north of the equator in just under eight hours. We stepped from the plane into an oven! The Robert Cobb family met us. Eddie Ziemann, Mission Chairman, was there from Takoradi. Everett Phillips, from Mission Headquarters in Missouri, was with him. Wow! Rev. Phillips had ushered me out of Ghana when I was forced to return to America in 1960. There he was to welcome me back! When he and I were trying to work around my physical problems in the early '60s, I doubt if either of us believed I would be back in Africa. It was emotionally overwhelming!

Rev. Phillips was in Africa to help get food to the Christians in Biafra, Nigeria, where people were starving because of war. Timing had made it a special day for Ann and me. Our mail from the USA was waiting. One letter was from my Aunt Leonora and Uncle Nevin in Phoenix, Arizona. I had addressed my farewell envelope to, *"Rev. & Mrs. E.N. Wister."* My uncle replied:

> *Now I've been called many things,*
> *But never yet a preacher.*
> *How the good Lord must grit his teeth*
> *To think, that awful creature!*
> *So, if a preacher I must be*
> *I guess I'll take my licking,*
> *But I expect invited out*
> *Each Sunday for fried chicken.*

I replied with a poem:

> *So that's what you think of a preacher,*
> *A not too desirable leecher!*
> *Your mate, I'm sure, would despair of life,*
> *If she should end up a preacher's wife.*
> *I admit to somewhat a mistake,*
> *But there are yet worse I could make.*

One that might leave you less merry,
Lo, to dub you a missionary!"

Eddie Ziemann took us to register at the American Embassy and appropriate Ghana organizations. We both registered as nurses to work in Ghana and I as a midwife. Our USA driver's licenses had not expired so we were not required to take the practical test to get our Ghana ones. For that we were grateful, as they still drove on the left side of the roads. I had *been there, done that,* but a few years ago! Driving left was very new to Ann. Two days later, we rode three hours in a Mercedes Benz to Takoradi. That was my first *air-conditioned* ride in Africa; I voted for it forever more!

Around one sharp curve, there sat a bus afire. Ann was being initiated to the unexpected. People were wailing as they ran in all directions. Both back wheels of the bus, still on the axle, were about a city block behind it in the gutter. People were burned, but there seemed to be none dead. Baggage atop the bus was burning; some may have lost every earthly possession. We stopped, but the police soon directed the traffic to pass. Around another bend, there was a police roadblock. Road work was being done. Women were selling shrimp kabobs. Eddie stopped and bought tree-ripened oranges for each of us. He bought two skewers of deep-fried shrimp. He gave one to the policemen on duty. Then he slipped a shrimp off the other skewer for each of us.

I had been gone so long. Situations were coming back, but slowly. The money system had changed. It had once been the pound, shilling, and pence like in England, then cedi and pesewa. We were now dealing in the percentile new cedi and new pesewa, almost equal to the American dollar and cents.

Takoradi was, as I remembered it, like a Garden of Eden with trees, flowers, and grass to the edge of the Gulf of Guinea. It was Ghana's first port city. The Zanes Shipping Company said our freight should arrive in Takoradi any day on the ship *Del Norte*. Ruby's Beautiful Blue, as she called her pickup, was there waiting for us. My VW was to have been ready at Brisco, a Swiss company, by January 14. Neither our goods nor my car came, so we drove the pickup north. This was sounding too familiar! My driving the pickup all over Takoradi on the left side of the streets made it feel comfortable and normal again. Ann's West Texas Youth Department had paid STL an amount to purchase and refurbish Ruby's Beautiful Blue; *we were grateful.*

On January 17, 1969, we drove through the coastal hills and then the lush African Ashanti Forest (jungle) to Kumasi. Vernon and Maxine Driggers, with their two teenagers, Verla and Bradley, were the missionaries in that huge city. Ann and I stayed in the strangers' house (guesthouse) across the lawn from the main house. Ann only stopped writing letters when the bell rang for a meal. I had done the same almost fifteen years before. On Sunday, we went to the huge Kumasi Assembly. It was high upon a hill where it became a landmark that helped me drive in Kumasi. What a colorfully dressed congregation! How they could sing and worship! I knew some of their worship words and sang along as I could. Lebanese friends brought lunch to the Driggers and stayed to eat. Ann and I were introduced to hummus, a garbanzo bean dip for pita bread, which they also brought. The rest of the delicious meal was explained to us as we ate.

On Monday, we took a guided tour through the vast Kumasi Hospital and Training School. I was interested that part of it seemed to be connected for credits to the University of Science and Technology about five miles from downtown Kumasi. The guide estimated the number of people lined up that day for treatment at three thousand. We were told they would pass through quickly. Like Ruby Johnson, I wondered if anyone knew whether each person was even warm and breathing. I have come to wonder this in America when doctors or HMOs allot fifteen minutes per client.

At the largest outdoor market and lorry-park in Kumasi, a policeman stopped us and said, "Get out of your truck!" I got! He directed me to the back of the truck and showed me a number broken on the license plate. When I explained that we had just taken possession of the truck, he just said, "Have it repaired!" I said, "Yes, Sir," and we drove on. The day was a stimulating glut of information to eye, ear, nose, taste, and touch! Ann's reaction to newness and their reaction to Ann was part of my enjoyment. That night we went to bed exhausted, but talked until after midnight.

On Tuesday, January 21, we drove north to Tamale where Hal and Naomi Lehmann met us. They were certainly sage veterans! It was difficult for me to see them without their daughter, Gretchen; she had always been there. Hal and Naomi Lehmann were commuting the eleven miles to Kumbungu to teach classes at NGBI. Bonnie Roll and Peggy Scott were living in the Tamale guesthouse. They had been living in the Yendi house while traveling to promote Sunday schools, youth department, and literature. However, Anne and Becky were soon coming from England to live in the Yendi house. Ann and I drove the eleven miles north from Tamale to the Northern Ghana Bible Institute at Kumbungu. Ann Fisher from west Texas met the McCorkles from south Texas. Franklin and Aneice McCorkle were teaching and directing the school. They had left their daughter, Amonna Sue, in America to attend higher education. Almost every day, Ann was meeting a new group of people. Déjà vu-- been there, done that. I was enjoying memories. Someone had been keeping my two guns registered. They were rusted from storage, so I cleaned and oiled them. It gave me something to do. My 0.22 rifle was to kill snakes, rabbits, and single big birds. The 410 shotgun was for flocks.

While we were in Tamale, Eddie Ziemann phoned. There was a dock strike in Houston; our freight had not even left the USA! We decided good things could come of this! The tires and tubes we had ordered from Sears for Ann's pickup could arrive in Houston and come in time to be added to our shipment. Our families and churches in Kansas, New Mexico, and west Texas had asked about sending extra barrels to Houston to come with the load. We were notified to pay extra for crating and loading those late items before anything would be shipped. Eddie sent them the money! On Wednesday, it seems everyone in Tamale helped to get Ruby's thirty drums plus some crates on a truck to be taken to Saboba. Ruby had gone home because of cancer; she had indicated that whoever went to Saboba should use her stored freight and aging canned goods. We got out the pages of instructions on onionskin paper she gave us in the USA; she wanted certain items saved for her. How grateful we were to have her things available and, at that moment, we did not know just how grateful we would become.

Ann and I went shopping for staples in Tamale on Thursday and left for Saboba by noon on Friday. We had a flat tire. A lorry driver stopped and helped to put on our spare. The delay caused us to arrive in Saboba about 9 P.M. on January 23 and there was no rousing welcome; everyone was asleep! Finally, two men, Biyimba and Abraham, came to help us get into the house and light a kerosene lamp. By that time, Ann looked quite in shock. She could not picture the house as I could, after Helen and I made it livable. The next day was different; people came to greet us all day long. Someone dashed us a chicken and a duck. We cooked them, as we were leaving again in a few days.

Some very disappointing news met us. The locals told us the hospital in Yendi was closed during the time the Russian Communists were dominating Ghana. We had no medical officer in Yendi who would be checking on Saboba Clinic. The nearest hospital or medical officer was one hundred miles away in Tamale. That posed two problems. Our work as nurse practitioners would not be supervised as closely and help would be over twice as far away for emergencies we could not handle. An example of this situation had happened the week before we reached Saboba. Makambi, the little mother who carried her pregnancies through an umbilical hernia, went into labor. We had successfully delivered several of her babies. This time the family tried to transport her all the way to Tamale, but she died before they reached the hospital. This put a guilt trip on us for being a week too late! She may or may not have survived had we been there. She was one great lady. I hope she acknowledged Jesus, the Son of God, as her Sacrifice and made Him Lord of her life, for I want to meet her again.

Inventory had to be taken at house and clinic. We got out the lists Hilda mailed to us and started on Saturday, but progress was slow. Happy people kept coming to welcome us. The weather was brutally hot! A woman glows; a man sweats. Whatever! Our clothing was soaked and water ran off our bodies. We longed for the snow on the New York runway! The diesel generator refused to spark, so we had no fan. Later in the day, when Mr. Kofi Mensah and his truck arrived with Ruby's barrels, he had a story to tell. The police had stopped him to check for license and insurance. Apparently, they were not in order, so we had to go to the police and verify the contents. The police said they would have confiscated the whole thing except they and the people had been waiting so long for medical aid. The Saboba Clinic and the Yendi Hospital had both been closed *over a year*! No wonder the men had been telling us to, "Hurry!"

Amos Biyimba, whom I had taught to cook years before, wanted his job again. We gladly hired him. Abraham Kusasi had worked for the previous nurses and been watchman while no one was in Saboba. We decided to continue to employ him for the yard work at least until we had time to evaluate his work. Biyimba, Abraham, and many others met the lorry and helped to unload Ruby's metal drums into our garage. We were using Ruby's truck and eating her canned goods. How God provides is usually amazing, and beyond our understanding! During the cleaning process in one room, we found a termite nest bigger than a #3 galvanized washtub. We were not sure which wall might collapse without that lost support. The whole house was a total disaster of mud and rock. I could see why Ruby said, "There must be a new house or present-day nurses will not live there." Pastor E. J. Namyela commented, "I do not know when or if you will make this so you can live in it."

We stopped everything and went to church on Sunday. What a welcome it was! They were dressed for Christmas! We were each asked to bring greetings. As expected, they asked about Ruby Johnson and the other nurses. Before and after the service they were showing me children who had been born since I left Saboba. Rev. E. J. Namyela Panka was pastor of the Toma church at the western edge of Saboba. He and his family were living in the house where Dewey Hale lived when we built the Toma Church thirteen years before; it was about a mile from our house. Pastor Namyela Panka, Karen, and their first three children, Susanna, Priscilla, and Gideon, had lived at Bunkpurugu, thirty miles east of the Nakpanduri Clinic, where I was stationed when I was ill and left Ghana in 1960. He was one of those beaten along with me in 1959. Then, while I was in the USA, he had been imprisoned for *political incorrectness* when communism dominated Ghana. After release, he felt it best to move from Bunkpurugu, so they came to pastor the Toma Church in Saboba.

When Ann and I got to Saboba, I met Deborah, Claudia, and Blondena, their children who had been born during my absence. The General Council consisted of the Northern and Southern Districts. While I was in the USA, E. J. Namyela was elected Superintendent of the Northern Ghana District Council. In early 1968, Rev. Eddie Ziemann, a missionary, was elected Superintendent of the General Council. Rev. E. J. Namyela was elected Assistant Superintendent, so he really held two positions besides Saboba Pastorate.

In about 1949, the Assemblies of God were invited to enter Saboba because of two things, Akonsi Konkomba, the

first Christian, and our medical help. Ann and I got to Saboba
in early 1969. By then, the Catholic Church had a technical
school down by the Ghana Government primary and middle schools. The Presbyterian Church was promoting agri-
culture, using water from the lake formed by a dam Dewey
Hale had promoted. Various tribes, even from Nigeria, were
involved in education, politics, marketing, and religion. British Wycliffe translators, Mary Steel and Mary Abbott, a midwife, were living in the local government guesthouse. They
were putting Lekpakpaln, the Konkomba language, into
writing. I had gone to SIL (Summer Institute of Linguistics)
at the University of Oklahoma since my first term in Saboba,
but we could not do justice to both medical and language.
All Assembly Missionaries in Saboba had worked on a songbook, using International Phonetics. Gylima Akonsi helped
me write the last song, *When the Roll is Called up Yonder*. ("Bi
Ya Ti Yi Ti Yimbil Paatcham.") I delivered the papers to Hal
Lehmann at the Tamale press as I was leaving on furlough in
1957. Wheeler and Eileen Anderson did the actual printing.
Now when Ann Fisher and I arrived in Saboba, we were told
that all three Christian churches in Saboba were using that
songbook. It felt good to know I had contributed. The first
Christian, Akonsi Konkomba, had paved the way for all this
change when he asked for medical help from the Assemblies of God. The Wycliffe ladies chose the Toma Assembly
as their home church. Gradually, the expatriates in Saboba
were having a meal with us, or vice-versa, to get to know
one another. A Brother at the Catholic Technical School was
American; we celebrate the Fourth of July and Thanksgiving
with him. We learned there was a Saboba Town Council and
the Chairman was not a Konkomba. I doubt the Konkombas would have tolerated that during my early years there;
Saboba, and Ghana, were changing.

As tired as we were and unsettled as our house was,
Ann and I returned to Tamale. The Northern Ghana District
Council met for business the first five days of February at the

Northern Ghana Bible Institute (NGBI) in Kumbungu. Four area pastors joined us for the one hundred eleven-mile journey; it was required. Within ten miles a tire blew. We put on the spare. More pastors joined us in Yendi. Between Yendi and Tamale, a tire went flat from a nail. We sat four hours in the hot sun while one pastor went on a passing lorry to have the tire patched and brought back on another lorry. From habit, we had water with us. Our freight with two Sears tires had not arrived. We were a bit amused that two Americans in West Africa were buying truck tires made in Communist China!

At the Council, I met Pastor John Kombet from Nakpanduri area. He had been among those beaten in Najong #2 a few years before, along with Pastor Namyela and me. Pastor John told me there was a new and larger church in Najong now. He said some of the ones who beat us had become Christians and one was the Superintendent of their Sunday school. He said the pastors in the Bimoba Section had been waiting until I could attend to dedicate the new church. While we were in Tamale, Ann wrote her first impressions in a letter to my parents:

> I have been at Saboba about a week and I guess you have heard it is not quite like my home in Texas, but I like it already. I'm just glad to unpack my suitcase for a few days! Within a week, we returned to Tamale for this Prayer Conference and District Council. It is inspirational! I've met new friends, both missionaries and Africans. I especially enjoy the open markets. People, food, flies, and clothing all mixed together. I've eaten all sorts of food like plantain and shrimp deep-fried in coconut oil, rice or yams flavored with beef, sheep, or goat gravy, all hot with peppers. Americans should be more thankful to God for water, among other things taken for granted! We hope our freight gets here soon. Write me! Anybody! Everybody! Love, Ann

The last night of the council, we were in committee meetings until midnight. By morning, I was vomiting and had a 104F degree temperature from malaria. Hal and Naomi Lehmann and Ann took the pastors back to Saboba, as they needed to be in their churches for Sunday. Ann was violently ill by the time she and the Lehmanns returned. She was unable to keep down the pills needed for treatment, so we gave her injections to stop the parasites. There were no disposable syringes and needles at the pharmacy. One of Ruby's drums in Saboba was full of nothing but sterile disposable needles and syringes! I traced one down in a back alley, still sealed in a plastic bag. I also found a small box of crackers and felt they would be good for Ann. They cost over five dollars, so I went home and made toast for her.

As soon as Ann could travel, we visited a few stations where Ann had not been. We ate lunch sixty miles north of Tamale at Walewale with Arthur and Doris Hockett from Houston, Texas. They had never met; it is a *furr-piece* from Lubbock to Houston in Texas! On the way to Bawku we made a side trip to Navrongo, where crocodiles were protected. The keepers allowed us to watch them feed chickens to the crocs. Two of the young men grabbed me and pulled me to the water's edge, pretending to feed me to the crocodiles! At Bawku, near the border to Burkina Faso (Upper Volta), I introduced Ann to Adeline Wichmann and Pauline Smith, aka Addie and Polly, aka A&P. Ann and I turned back southeast, forty miles to the Nakpanduri clinic station where I had lived in 1959–60. Eloise Smith and Ruth Anderson were the nurses there. They were due for furlough in the near future.

From there we returned to Saboba via the Gushiago moto'way, the dusty two-rut road that led us home to our mail and church on Sunday. In one letter, Mom said the mortgage company had increased the payment on my house; it was more than the rent she was receiving. I wrote Mountain States Mortgage Company, they reduced the payment and insurance from eighty-six to seventy-nine dollars per month.

On Sunday morning, we drove to Yankazia to greet the chief, U Na Febor Jayom, attend church, and meet their young pastor, Samson Abarika and his family. He was a Nanumba by tribe and had graduated from NGBI. We were late getting started to go the sixteen miles for a morning service. Ann wanted to drive. Of course she needed to become comfortable with driving on what we called the "talcum powder way;" the dust was so deep. Ann was going so slowly that I thought if she didn't drive faster, we were going to miss the whole church service. It seemed the more I said, the slower she got. Finally, I said, "Stop and let me drive! Otherwise we may as well go back home!" She did, but cried. As the Africans would say, "And did you learn anything?" I was supposed to be the mature one! I apologized, but later. It hurt me so deeply, that from then on I made sure that if I felt I had hurt her I would apologize immediately and not later! I reminded myself that I had once been the new one. She was doing so great, much better than most would have done at her age! I learned that she could be stubborn; that was her coping mechanism. She got quiet and said not a word, but didn't move. In most cases, the situation did not matter one way or another.

In years past, I was often told that I seemed to be able to fit in anytime, any place and with anyone because I usually didn't care. I had to think on this; had Africa changed me? I recalled some of Ruby Johnson's philosophy: "This *ABNORMAL EXISTENCE* in the bush, of two adult females having traveled thousands of miles and many hours together to an isolated, unknown location, far away from family and telephone, to administer a clinic together, be on call twenty-four hours a day, manage living quarters and eat together, serve an area of churches together, plan and supervise any construction, maintain transportation, and yet take care of each other when malaria or dengue fever struck and be expected to keep some kind of mutual admiration or respect—*is FOR THE BIRDS!*" In defense of the system, I found that I did develop a respect for my full-time nurse coworkers and their *specific calling*. I liked them better when we parted after three or four years than when we met, because I knew them better!

That evening Pastor Namyela went with us to the church in Gbenja, where we met Pastor Lekpamba's wife and family. He was a Konkomba by tribe and had graduated from NGBI. The Chief of that area was also a Christian. The church was near a home where, in late 1957, a woman had been ill and was brought to the clinic. When she got well, the Chief of the village had the people make a road so Gretchen Lehmann, a teenager, and I could go to his village for a service. The Gbenja church had since been built, but out closer to the main road. Now they had a pastor! On a Wednesday evening, we went to the dynamic, progressive church in Kokonzoli. There were a number of Spirit-filled young people and dedicated young families. Dahamani Dagomba was pastor. The mud church did not look safe to me. I told them what Ruby Johnson said about helping with a roof if they did the building. I helped the carpenter make forms to mold adobe bricks like in New Mexico. The aggressive group got busy making blocks for their new church.

We left workmen painting our house and drove as far as Tamale again. It was Thursday, February 20. We opened an account at the bank with our one hundred fifty-dollar monthly allowances. It had doubled since I first came in 1954! We received a letter saying that a percent would be deducted monthly from that allowance to pay for the food items in our barrels and the freight for shipping that food. We didn't even have it yet! We had been using most of our money for gasoline and tires, salary for helpers and even medication for the clinic! I had to forget about being the well-paid instructor at nursing schools. I never wanted to live and work just for shelter and food. To me that was not living, yet many in the world wish for just that. We shopped at Kingsway Pharmacy for medications to stock the clinic and ate lunch at the new Government Catering rest house. We mailed letters to USA churches, friends, and family.

On Friday, we parked the Beautiful Blue and took a plane to Kumasi where we had reservations at the new air-conditioned City Hotel. Ann sort of quietly made things like this happen to relax us. However, in former years there were no hotels in Kumasi. It rained the first day! We had not seen rain since the day we left Kumasi before. We expected our Volkswagen from Germany, provided by the New Mexico Youth Department, to be available by the time we got to Kumasi; it was not. We walked from the hotel to the conference site. The pickup was great as an ambulance and for building projects but it was death on sore backs and pocketbooks! Don and Dixie Cox, visitors from the USA, were guest speakers at the conference. Jim Kessler was voted in as Mission Chairman, separate from the Ghana Church. Jim and Delta had just returned to Ghana; Eddie and Bernice Ziemann were soon due for furlough.

After the three-day conference in Kumasi, Ann and I rode south with Jim and Delta Kessler to Tema. The harbor was built at Tema because of its rocky coastline rather than at the sandy beach at Accra. A true motorway, the only one in Ghana, ran twenty miles between Accra, the capitol, and Tema because of industry, like Lever Brothers, developing near the new Tema harbor. On Saturday morning, Ann and I tried to phone Texas and New Mexico. The line had only one opening for Monday; Ann booked that to Texas. In Saboba, one had to forget the phone was ever invented.

Pastor Tete, a Ghanaian, spoke on Sunday in both morning and evening services at the coastal Tema church. Nurses Eloise and Ruth, the Hokett family, and the two of us ate lunch with the Kesslers. That evening as we drove back to church along the beach, we stopped by the roadside for Pepsi and plantain chips freshly cooked in deep coconut oil over a campfire. On Monday morning, I gave Delta a perm while Ann went to the telephone office to talk with her family. At noon, we rode with the Kesslers to the Bob Cobb family home in Accra for lunch. Bonnie and Peggy were there from Tamale. Eddie and Bernice Ziemann came from Takoradi with good and bad news. Our new Wee Dubya had come, but our personal freight was still in Houston! We returned to Takoradi with the Ziemanns. They stopped in Saltpond where Oliver and Peggy Swain were teaching at the Southern Bible School. Ann made a big hit with the young students; both men and women were training to become pastors and Christian workers.

In Takoradi, we found our little white car with the bright new license tags truly waiting for us. We had told the Konkombas in Saboba that we would get the Volkswagen and be back in about two weeks. It was more like a month! We were finally on our way to Saboba with one more item checked off the waiting list. We drove north through Kumasi, Mampong, Yeji, and Salaga. At Yeji, we crossed Lake Volta, the largest man-made lake in the world. It covers over 3,275 square miles, four percent of Ghana's total surface. Over fifty towns had to be resettled almost immediately. The Akosombo Dam, eighty miles north of Accra-Tema, gradually formed the Volta Lake. I believe the USA had an interest in the initial building of the dam, whether engineering, financing, or both. Water has even backed up into the Oti River almost to Bimbila, about one hundred miles south of Saboba. A loop of the Oti River surrounds Saboba, forty miles north of Yendi where we get our mail. The first time Helen Kopp and I crossed the Volta River at Yeji in 1954, it took longer for workers to load the barge than to cross the river. When Ann Fisher and I crossed in the VW in 1969, it took nearly an hour to cross after all vehicles and passengers were on the ferry. They were telling the drivers of the big trucks they would have to wait an hour for the ferry that was coming from the other side. When they saw our little VW, they motioned us to drive into a small spot. They would not allow us to sit in our car. We were late so all benches were taken. We tried to find shade near the huge trucks, but the heat was sickening in March. It was cooler in the middle of the lake.

In Tamale, we went shopping for last minute items not available in Saboba. We hired a fitter (mechanic) to work on our light plant. On March 14, I drove the VW to Saboba. Ann drove the pickup and took along the fitter. The thermometer on our porch in Saboba read 130F degrees! Since the diesel engine was still not working, we had not even a fan. I had never had electricity in Saboba, but the engine was there so why not use it? We scanned some of our mail collected as we passed through Yendi. In one letter Mom wrote that their TorC pastors, Rev. and Mrs. Hill had resigned and moved to Alamogordo to semi-retire and be near their daughter, Janice. The Kenneth Smiths came to pastor the TorC church, where they met my mom. They had already been supporting me in Africa. They later went as missionaries to Latin America.

When we arrived back in Saboba, the Konkombas were about ready to throw us to the wild animals, so they said. We had been gone too long, had not paid our workers the first of the month, and arrived with no cash to pay them! We knew we would be returning the fitter to Tamale and could get the money. He got the lights to come on in Ann's room and the clinic, but the bats had chewed the wires in the main house and the kitchen. We would still use some Kerosene lamps. We took the fitter back to Tamale the same day. He drove the VW partway to Tamale that evening and it did not take three hours! Ann, in the back seat, said she started to tell me to roll up my window so she would not fly out. The driver seemed to be in control of his vehicle, but did not try to miss the bumps! It tested my fused spine. Among other things, we got the money to pay workers.

Before March 27, when we planned to open the clinic, we took the four Konkomba Area pastors and the six from

Yendi Section to a routine pastors' meeting eighty miles south to Pusuga. Until Anne Symonds and Becky Davison came from furlough in England, we were helping pastors in both sections. I had been to these villages with Dewey Hale when he showed me towns his plane flew to for clinics and church. I had even slept one night at Zabzugu or Pusuga years ago. Through it all, Ann Fisher and I were so tired that we felt ill with a low-grade fever most of the time. It was probably from traveling, sorting through Ruby's drums, cleaning, and remodeling house and clinic. We decided that Paludrin for malarial prophylaxis was not effective, so we changed to Chloroquin. That is used to treat malaria, not as a prophylaxis, but it worked better. The few clouds made humidity high. The high temperatures plus the low-grade fever made us miserable day and night. Our beds and pillows were soaked with perspiration at afternoon naptime and at night.

At first, the Ghanaians had trouble understanding Ann's Ameri-Tex-English; she had trouble with their British English. On my first arrival to Africa, I came straight from fourteen months in England so did not experience that as much. I adjusted in England! Another interesting gap was about equipment like the kerosene fridge, wringer washing machine, and flatirons that were new to the Africans. They thought most people in America probably had them. Ann had skipped them! She was born into an era of electricity, running water, and automatic washers and dryers with permanent press clothing! In late March, Ann explained this in a letter to my parents:

> In the USA you usually don't think of washing clothes
> as an all-day job, but out here it is a major project. This
> morning, after Biyimba heated the water on a wood
> stove, Abraham, our yardman, sparked the diesel gener-
> ator. Charlese plugged in the wringer washing machine
> and we went to work! Wow! I leave the flatirons and
> charcoal iron for Biyimba, our house helper. I am glad

Charlese knows about kerosene refrigerators. I have learned to light the kerosene lamps and blow them out. This has been a big jigsaw puzzle! Today I helped Biyimba cook lunch on a wood stove in a kitchen attached to the garage so it doesn't make the main house hot. The duck wouldn't bake; the water boiled over. Maybe there is still hope for me; I try hard. A short rain shower came today, the first I've seen in Saboba. It cooled the weather some. I have started working with the CAs (youth) at church. We are busy!

Love and prayers, Ann

In so many ways, Ann was opposite to Helen Kopp, my first coworker. Helen wore her pith helmet religiously, as she did her mosquito and snake boots at sundown, and used the net over her bed. Ann did not like the traditional pith helmet and she wore thongs or regular shoes. She had a mosquito net over her bed, but didn't always use it. I used my mosquito net regularly, usually wore a straw hat, but joined Ann in wearing *thongs*. (Flip-flops are called thongs in Africa.) We did boil our water and take malarial prophylaxis each morning.

At first, it was best that I have the one bedroom in the main house so I could answer callers coming to the door day and night for a variety of situations. Ann had the extra bedroom Ruby built and could dress it up a bit. From her room she could come along a cement walk to enter the screened porch of the main house. The window from the porch into my bedroom, which Helen and I had once climbed through, had been cut down to floor level as a door. Ann usually entered the main house, still a fishbowl, through that door into my bedroom and on through an arched door to the living room. The lights in Ann's bedroom came on when Abraham sparked the diesel engine and it provided electricity from about 6 P.M. to 9 P.M. She could plug in a fan for that short time, but returned to perspiration and a wet bed soon after the engine was killed each night. Ruby had put in a flush toilet and a small septic tank in the new bedroom. Outside that bedroom was a tower holding a barrel into which water could be pumped from a barrel on the ground. That way, the toilet could be flushed lightly, but the pump was not working. She flushed that toilet by pouring a bucket of water into it. We took boiled water from the fridge each evening to brush our teeth. Our freight had not come so in the main house, we still used the cong-cong (noisy tin can), guz-zunder, and sand box, whatever! At least they worked! Septic tanks had to be cleaned at times. The one behind the kitchen needed cleaning when we got there; it overflowed with the rains. There was also a cement cistern behind the kitchen to collect rainwater. A pump pulled the water up out of the cistern into a higher barrel and sent running water into the kitchen, but that pump did not work!

I worked on old clocks, water filters, water pumps, a shower spray, an eggbeater, a blood pressure cuff, and other items to exhume them from their tropical death! I decided modernized items were useless; there was good and bad to progress! I voted for kerosene lamps and a good bucket to get water from the well!

1. Ann and me; York, England with Phyllis Jones Dec. 1968. 2. Ghana Airways—London to Accra. 3. Bernice (and Eddie, chairman) Ziemann, Takoradi. 4. Saboba house (before and after) Ruby Johnson (second bedroom far left.) 5. Ann unpacking. 6-7. Dorcas Njonibi in and holding pan. 8. (L-R) Engine room, bungalow, kitchen and store room, Turner Ch. (far), 2-car garage, library (far) 1971. 9-10. VW, Biyimba, clinic (far), Chev and three pastors in water. 11. Yardman Abraham at clothesline. Their new quarters are behind double garage.

CHAPTER TWO

Tribal War in Yendi
New Church in Najong #2

ON TUESDAY, APRIL 1, the clinic officially opened. The Regional Medical Officer arrived from Tamale. We had a reception with tea and goodies for twenty dignitaries from Tamale, Yendi, and Saboba. During the process, we voiced our concern of how dangerous it was for sick people to travel one hundred miles to Tamale rather than forty miles to Yendi for emergency medical help. Local chiefs, Saboba town officials, policemen, teachers from primary, middle, and technical schools, and members from the other three missions in the area supported our plea. Officials responded and the Yendi hospital eventually reopened with Dr. Korsah as District Medical Officer. His father was once Attorney General of Ghana. We proudly showed the visitors through the medical supply room, general clinic treatment rooms, and the maternity facilities. The waiting shed to protect patients from the sun needed repair. The round mud huts, behind the main clinic, had mostly fallen down. They were used for families with a member being treated for snakebite or other serious problem. We appealed for help from chiefs and local council members to rebuild those. The clinic walls were rock and cement, not rock and mud as in our residence. Yet rats, termites, lizards, spiders, blowing dust, and general disuse contributed to its erosion when closed.

Wednesday, April 2, was prenatal day and the first official day of clinic treatment. We evaluated fourteen expectant mothers. Leper treatment was now done by a government agency, so we had general outpatient clinic each weekday except Wednesday. That day was for the mothers and children. Another change was that *we charged a fee;* medicines were expensive. The maternity and general patients paid about fifteen cents (15NP) for the first visit, ten cents for return visits and twenty cents for injections. We sometimes did not charge the severe cases for the total number of injections they required.

The Ghanaians had discovered the swift and almost magical results of the injection, and would pay any price on the gray market for them. This often produced abscesses from dirty needles and syringes, while the medication may be only water. With Ruby's drum of disposable syringes, we did not have the problem of burning pans full of glass syringes, but had to prevent their use and reuse in the villages. Edward Dondow was the main full-time orderly. He was doing what Gylima, his wife's uncle, did when I was in Saboba before. Dundow interpreted for us as we examined the sick people and dispensed the medication we advised. He came to wake us at night for deliveries or any emergency.

How I missed Gylima! Someone had *sacked* him; they said he allowed his drinking to affect his work. I went to see him; he never came to the door. One day he ran when he saw me on a path; he must have been terribly hurt! Once I sent word that I was coming to visit him on a certain day. Even then, I had to *go-and-come* a few times before I saw him. He was so ill that I cried.

Charging fees forced us to hire local lads just out of middle school to collect money and keep records. Three such lads were Joshua Gewen Beso of Toma, Joel Ubor Wumbei of Yankazia, and Tege Tachin of Nalongni. That number increased as more completed middle school and we started evaluating them for future education. There were more applications than jobs. They helped Dondow pre-pack adult and child doses of medication and even interpret for us when he was too busy. We were interested in getting those educated who would someday work us out of our job. I foresaw a time when they would manage the clinics without us. An older man wrapped ulcers and worked in the yard. I nearly *sacked* him more than once, but kept him as he had a young family to feed.

∽ ∽ ∽

Easter was April 6, 1969. On Christian holidays, we tried to do something special with each church. We planned to be with the people in Kokonzoli for Good Friday evening, but a delivery kept us from going. Then a man came with his right hand almost cut off. We took him to Tamale. We went to Kokonzoli Saturday evening instead. When they saw the lights of our car, people came to the church from every direction. Ann told them how and why she came to be in Ghana. I gave greetings. As Rev. Namyela was speaking on the reason for Communion, people began to praise God in their heavenly language. It brought back memories of joy when I first experienced this as a teenager. I was not in the Saboba Area when so many received the Baptism in the Holy Spirit; Helen and Ruby wrote me about it. The younger people in Kokonzoli were fervent for their Lord!

The next morning we went for a Toma Church Sunrise Service at the top of a hill. Pastor Namyela and the people of the local Toma Church planned it and worshiped with the gifts of the Holy Spirit in operation. Blessed progress! Between the sunrise service and the Easter service at the church, we treated a small child who had tetanus (lockjaw).

Every aspect of our life was fragmented; that is how we lived.

We got to Toma Church for part of the morning service. Youngsters presented a skit to show how Jesus appeared to certain people after His death. On Sunday afternoon, the two Wycliffe Marys went with Ann and me to Yankazia, where Pastor Abarika had planned a communion service for Easter. How blessed to be with U Na Febor Jayum and the local Christians again. On our way back to Saboba, we stopped at the Gbenja Church, where I spoke. We helped Pastor Lekpamba serve Communion to his people; for some it was their first!

The Northern Ghana Bible Institute at Kumbungu opened on April 8, so it had been difficult for our missionary peers to attend the official opening of the Saboba Clinic. They had seen it open and close many times. The whole Executive Committee of the General Council came one week later. Our local Pastor Namyela was on that committee and had invited them to Saboba for the next meeting. We fed and lodged the missionaries. Pastor Namyela and his wife, Karen, found lodging for Ghanaians; local Christians provided food. Eddie Ziemann, an official, had come over five hundred miles from Takoradi and had severe chest congestion. As we toured them through the clinic, we found treatment for him. The day after they left, we had the first real tropical storm of the season. We saw the dark bank of clouds in the northeast; they were coming rapidly. We closed all the glass louvers; Ruby had replaced the wooden shutters and made it more of a fishbowl. The dust came first and then the rain. When it was over, we got barefoot and mopped up water and mud from our floors with terry towels and area rugs. In the next two days, we killed four snakes. We had seen so few snakes that Ann decided I was telling snake fables. The hot weather had kept them underground; the first heavy rain drove them out.

The first official deliveries at the clinic were, obviously, *walk-ins*. The women had neither seen a doctor nor obtained prenatal care during pregnancy. The first delivery produced a three-pound live, limp boy. Among the first seventeen deliveries, five could be considered *normal*! Two of the normal babies were girls, one for Ndamba Kayil and one Binganingma, both from Toma. Other complications in the newborn included low birth-weight and pre-maturity, stillbirth, a macerated fetus, and hydrocephaly. Two stillborn *followed* their placenta. The average weight of live infants was less than five pounds. We seldom saw a mother with hemoglobin of above forty percent. In mothers, we saw premature labor, early fatigue, and shock from hemorrhage in first, second, or third stage with a loss of 500 ml or more. The first and second stages were long because of breech, persistent posterior position, or a hand presenting with the head. Poor muscles tone contributed to this. The cord was often around the limp infant's neck. This could have been from stooping low for long periods of time in their farms. Frequent retained placentas in the third stage were removed manually. Precipitous deliveries occurred at home, on the road, or in the bathroom off the veranda of the clinic as some women refused to stay in the maternity ward.

This gave us copious material for prenatal classes and the situation did not improve quickly. After months of prenatal care (teaching classes, regular checkups, antibiotics, vitamins, iron, and folic acid) those statistics changed dramatically. Later we evaluated seventeen consecutive maternity cases to compare. All but two were normal, spontaneous deliveries. One was a pre-eclamptic with a live baby and uneventful sequel. We transported one mother for help because of disproportion; this resulted in a live mother and baby. By the end of April, we were treating fifty to seventy sick people, four times a week, in general outpatient clinic. When a clinic day fell on market day, every six days, that number might increase to one hundred. Maternity day attendance moved quickly to forty and more.

Ann insisted we go to Tamale for my birthday, May 3. We had letters to mail. One was to my maternal grandmother. My Mamaw, at eighty-four, still lived alone in a small house in TorC, New Mexico and wrote me quite often. Her oldest and youngest daughters, my mother and my aunt, lived in TorC. In Tamale, we were told that our freight had been shipped from Houston on the Del Mundo of the Delta line. We had been in Ghana six months. On my birthday, Ann left me sleeping and went shopping. She returned with a lovely gift of African cloth and had made reservations for Peggy and Bonnie to eat Indian curry with us at the Government Catering Resthouse. These are the kinds of special things Ann did quietly.

On one shopping day, we talked to a man at Tamale Public Works Department (PWD) about the diesel generator in Saboba. They did road repair, but they sometimes had generators at their facilities in remote areas. On his next day off, the man came to Saboba and replaced the electric wires to the kitchen and main mud house, including *my bedroom*. That completed my birthday! A PWD truck pumped out the septic tank behind the kitchen. The man repaired water pumps, so we had water coming from the pipes into the kitchen and Ann's room. For the bathroom in the main mud house, Abraham still climbed a ladder to pour the water in a high barrel as it was under a grass roof. That house would have to have a metal roof before we could funnel water into my bathroom. We finally had lights and fans for three hours each evening. We had music from a tape recorder and instead of the charcoal iron, Biyimba used an electric iron by sparking the diesel engine. We had spent a lot of money buying batteries for our tape recorders so we could have music; now we would use more diesel fuel! We could buy D.C. light bulbs in Ghana stores. To use A.C. electric-powered items brought from America, we must plug them into a portable eight-inch square transformer. Until our transformers came in our freight, we moved Ruby's one transformer around for priorities. When several arrived in our freight, we discovered those heavy things were hard on toes in the dark!

Back in Saboba, I made an Indian curry meal with Biyimba like the one we had in Tamale; we put it in his card file. I was delighted to have Biyimba back as our helper. He had a schedule at the house the same as helpers at the clinic. Biyimba cooked every day. He cleaned one of the four rooms thoroughly each day so that at the end of the week all rooms had been cleaned once. Tuesday was different; he filled the fridge with kerosene and evened the wick, changed the bed linen, and did the washing on the wringer machine. He soaked the beans Monday night, so they cooked each Tuesday on the wood fire that heated wash water. We helped with the washing when patient count was lower on Tuesdays. I learned from Biyimba that the Ghanaians also felt the frustration of being far from a major town. He had been farming before we came and his family lived over a mile from our house. He took time off to go to Tamale and order lumber and aluminum for building a house for his family nearer to his work. He returned, saying the man he went to see had gone south to Kumasi. He left a message along with a list of his needs. The man returned, got his message, and the building material arrived the following Sunday. Biyimba's many activities in the church were interrupted and he did not even like paying the man on Sunday! Still, he must care for his family. Ann and I visited one home on our way to church and saw how they coped with the March hunger season each year. The children were skinning the meat for the evening meal; it was six small rats and a snake about three feet long. They had no money to buy beef from the local butcher on market day as we did, but we had no time to hunt rats, snakes or rabbits. This brought the great American depression to mind; mother said we ate the seed beans, so had none to plant!

Soon after the birthday trip to Tamale, malaria attacked me again and I was violently ill for a week. During that time, a woman from Sanguli hemorrhaged and came to the maternity clinic. Dondow put a quilt on the clinic floor where I could lie down and yet support Ann as she delivered the baby. An arm presented along with the head; a loop of the cord dropped down and there was no pulse in it. The five-pound baby was born dead. I think the mother recovered more quickly than Ann did. She needed to see some normal cases and they were not happening. The next day, at noon, the previous scenario was repeated except I could at least stand up. A woman came from Sachal. The placenta came ahead of the three-pound stillborn with the shoulder presenting, while the mother bled. Ann attended every delivery with me unless she was too ill. That helped a lot during those first abnormal cases. She did the paper work, bathed, and observed the new baby while Dondow and I cared for the mother. These two cases gave us a clue that perhaps we should give penicillin to those who were near term and yet had never had prenatal care because of clinic closure. It would save some babies near full term. Later on, we would not do this unless the husband and other wives, if he had more than one, would all receive and pay for injections simultaneously. This helped whole families in future pregnancies.

As if we were not busy enough, we started language lessons with Gideon Tadimie Jagir of Kpatapaab, Chief Quadin's village. Gideon had just completed middle school. They usually took their father's first name for their last name. Tadimie's father, Jagir, was a picturesque, senior gentleman in his northern Ghana hat and he was a member of Chief Quadin's Council. I recalled that during our first time in Saboba, Gylima Akonsi was our clinic helper, language teacher, interpreter at the church, and usually led the congregational singing. Sometimes Teacher Samson Mankrom led the singing. Those jobs were now divided among many, but I never stopped missing Gylima. Dondow, Deacon Beso's son-in-law, had been trained for the clinic job while I was in America. I found him as capable and dedicated to the clinic as Gylima was.

After a busy general clinic on a Friday in mid-May, we were writing. It was market day and a lorry driver could take our letters to Yendi. Suddenly there was a loud clapping of hands at our door. It was Pastor Namyela. The wife of Oyum had been struck by lightning; the couple attended the Toma Church. She had been helping to repair their house and had an iron wedge in her hand when struck. The local belief is that whatever you have in your hand when you are struck by lightning, you have stolen. We rushed to a house near Maja's house, just before going up the steep west hill. We injected a sedative as the woman was still convulsing. We noted two streaks were burned on her upper lip as if fire had gushed from her nose. Her hand was burned. It was difficult to evaluate vital signs, even pulse and respiration. Pastor Namyela prayed with the family. When we were sure the woman recognized us, we left. Every day we went to inject vitamins until she was eating well. The woman said she had stolen nothing and proved it by surviving. Most people struck by lightning had not survived to prove their innocence.

When we got back to our house, a noisy palaver was taking place. A pig was loose in our yard and eating one baby chick after another. An African fell atop the pig and killed it. We knew neither who owned the pig nor who ate it. A huge dark cloud descended on Saboba and all ran to their house. The storm ended the local market and people fled every direction for home. Our clinic helper came with a man who had cut off a finger while fishing. The finger was gone; three others were almost off. We repaired his hand the best we could, as he did not want to go to Yendi. We never got back to our letter writing; we went to bed!

Early the next morning a woman came to the clinic bleeding profusely. We took her to Yendi, without the letters we planned to write on market day. We were late to Yankazia for the usual Saturday clinic. Few people were waiting, as most people were in their fields planting because of the rain the day before. We went back to Saboba and wrote letters by hand or on a portable machine borrowed from the Lehmanns. The man whose wife had been struck by lightning came to dash us a chicken for helping his family. A calm quiet rain came with no wind, sand, or lightning. That meant the true rainy season had started; it was cooler. The next Sunday we went to Gbenja for morning service, where I gave the Word. Then we walked with Pastor Lekpamba to a village he said he felt strongly urged to visit. We walked about two miles and asked a headman permission to have a service. Pastor gave God's Word and seven people came forward to accept Christ as their means of salvation. Pastor said he would go back many times to teach them from God's Word. We had not planned for that trek, so my only shade was my Bible balanced atop my head. I got sunburned!

Finally, at the clinic, two normal deliveries happened simultaneously, one on a Saturday night and another three hours later on Sunday morning. We missed the morning service at the local church. Already, with two months of good prenatal care, we were seeing more deliveries that were normal. To welcome the new wee ones was becoming a joy rather than a dread!

Sunday evening we decided to go to the Kokonzoli Church. It was on an alternate route to Yendi. We planned to take the key to the Yendi mission bungalow and leave it with someone in Yendi. Anne Symonds and Becky Davison were due to arrive from England any day and would need it. From then on, we had to specify the Saboba Ann or the Yendi Anne. We stopped in Kokonzoli to greet Pastor Dahamani and planned to return in time to attend his evening church service. He told us the road was bad and suggested that two family men from the church go with us. Before we got to the next village of Demon, the VW was having trouble in the deep, sticky mud. We did go-and-come, as the Africans say, but it took us longer than planned. In the process, I shot two rabbits. A shell jammed or I would have had the third! (A true sportsman, "The big one got away!") Because of the rain, I thought we would see fowl, so I took only my shotgun. In my haste, I did not brace well, so the next day my shoulder was black. We felt proud to bring meat to the Kokonzoli Pastor.

When we arrived, a group met us with one big palaver. One man came to the car all bloody. He said, "I have a case; your pastor has struck me!" He was the teacher from the Kokonzoli primary school. We forgot the rabbits and sat down to hear the palaver. Many young men in the local Assembly of God had donated labor to build the local primary school with supplies provided by the Ghana Government. The supervisor of the building project had even chosen to stay in the parsonage, where it was comfortable. The schoolteacher arrived later. When the Assembly of God building fell down completely, the teacher made the decision that they could not meet temporarily in the school building on Sundays, so the scene was set. While we were gone to Yendi, the teacher had thrown the final insult at Pastor Dahamani. He accused him, as a bachelor, of making advances toward his sister. The pastor said he had been so careful and could tolerate no more abuse. He split the teacher's lip. The members of the church were standing behind Pastor Dahamani solidly. Saboba Ann was learning what it meant to hear a palaver. As you hear each side, you think they might come to blows again.

Finally, I said, "Well, of course a pastor should never strike any person. However, our pastors have been called of God and have prepared many years. They should be respected by local villagers."

Then I suggested that we bring District Superintendent Rev. N. Panka to Kokonzoli the next day, since he did live in Saboba and he knew the African customs better than I did. The teacher agreed. The next morning Ann managed the clinic alone. Pastor Namyela and I drove to Kokonzoli. Pastor Namyela insisted on asking the girl if the accusations were true. She said Pastor Dahamani was innocent; both men reluctantly apologized. We took the teacher to Saboba clinic, gave him penicillin, a tetanus injection, and pain medication, and dressed the lip. We took him back to Kokonzoli; I hope someday he joined that church.

When it was time for pastors' meeting on Thursday, May 29, we collected pastors in Ruby's Beautiful Blue (now Ann's) and drove to Yendi again. There we learned that Rev. Bechi, Tamale Assembly pastor, had died and we were to be there Sunday, June 1, for a memorial service. They buried people immediately because of the heat and lack of refrigeration, but had a memorial service later. We took Saboba and Yendi Area pastors to Tamale for that funeral and returned them immediately after.

June was the sixth month since we arrived in Ghana, so we decided to evaluate our efforts.

1) Our house had been repaired and was livable. Going thorough this the second time exacerbated my frustration, and fatigue gave both of us malaria that otherwise we might have avoided. Same song, second verse--been there, done that! *We needed a new house!*

2) Six months and our freight still had not come. The man in the USA who was making a camper shell for Ann's pickup had a heart attack and it wasn't coming at all. This proved my theory that "things were happening to us that started out to happen to somebody else!"

3) The clinic had been open two months and we had treated 1,404 people. That included about one snakebite per week. We tended eleven deliveries, most with severe problems.

4) We taught Religious Education classes each week in the government schools. The boys and girls were so special because of their potential; we got to know them! We even treated one schoolboy for snakebite.

5) The building programs were forced upon us in two ways, by growth in numbers of believers and by erosion of buildings. Church and clinic buildings had fallen down. Volunteers were making blocks in three villages. The local Toma Church planned to build Sunday school rooms; Yankazia and Kokonzoli were planning new church buildings. On the first Saturday of June, Ann went for Yankazia clinic and returned to report the roof had blown off that little clinic. Part of the walls went with it and the storm had soaked whatever equipment, supplies, and medications we kept there. This was a good time of year to make adobe brick as the weather was cooler for working and the rains, still light, provided water. Otherwise, the people walked to the river for water or we hauled it in metal drums in the pickup from the earthen dam Dewey Hale promoted years before. Brick makers in villages were begging for our empty metal packing drums to collect water in and we had only a few of Ruby's empty. It could also be difficult if rains were heavy and washed away new bricks, roads and bridges.

6) Toma's Pastor Namyela was progressive. He worked with Bonnie Roll and Peggy Scott toward a Gold Crown Sunday School and a strong youth group. The Toma Sunday School attendance averaged over one hundred fifty. Both the women and men's fellowships were organized; he encouraged all area churches and pastors to do likewise. Ann, being younger, was working with the local CAs and a choir at Toma Church. Groups at the outstation were asking her to help them organize. She

started with Yankazia Church, as we had a clinic there each Saturday.

7) The garden seed in my barrels had not come in time to be planted. I planted old beans; they didn't come up. In my last minutes in America, I put packets of lettuce and tomato seed in my suitcase. We were eating leaf lettuce and the tomato plants were up.

8) In the middle of June, we were required to go to the coast for a meeting of nurses in Accra. We stayed a few days at Takoradi to rest. We were terribly tired from the heat, repairing our living quarters while living in it, and facing many complicated deliveries. We took a plane from Tamale; we felt too tired to drive. We were home again by the end of June.

I had not successfully raised the total amount of money quoted to build a new house in Saboba for us nurses. The project was never mentioned at conferences; it seemed not the right time to pursue it. I decided to get permission to buy cement for the adobe blocks and corrugated tin to replace grass roofs on the church buildings and clinic buildings going up. The buildings would last longer in the heavy, tropical rains and wind. I wrote to church officials at NMDC and Everett Phillips in Springfield about money from my account for six projects:

- language study (ten dollars per month);

- cement and tin roofing for three area churches (three hundred dollars);

- two hundred bundles of grass around 50NP to top the tin roof of our own house to make it cooler inside;

- help for national workers to attend the West African Conference in Kumasi in September (one hundred fifty dollars);

- help toward a hostel for missionary children at a school in Jos, Nigeria, and in Ivory Coast (two hundred dollars);

- a septic tank for Saboba mud house, since a new house seemed to be impossible (one hundred dollars).

Among our mail from home was a letter from Mrs. Earl Vanzant, Director of the women's department at NMDC. She said the ladies of New Mexico were sending a drum of clinic items with another missionary's freight in about six months. In another letter, we received the belated news that my last nephew, Darrin Lee, was born May 17, in Seattle. As usual when I was in Africa, I would wait years to see him! Mom was the typical doting grandmother and Dad, while appearing not to be too impressed, raced to see every grandchild ASAP!

On July 2, Ann stayed by herself overnight for the first time since our arrival. I made a trip to the Baptist Hospital in Nalerigu. It was a four-hour trip, as the rains had washed out the roads. We had three medical problems to discuss with their doctors. We took a boy who had a nerve condition like cerebral palsy. As it happened, they could not help him. We took Helen, the daughter of our head clinic worker, Dondow. She was crippled by polio. They told us about a rehab hospital in Accra where Helen could be evaluated. We took a pastor for examination of a hernia. He was given a future date for surgery. When we returned to Saboba, I learned that a policeman had gone to our bungalow after he saw my car leave town. He made Ann feel threatened and she had some difficulty convincing him to leave. She called for Abraham, our Kusasi yardman, to come ASAP and the policeman left! She got Ruthie and Gretchen, our cook's two oldest daughters, to sleep at our house that night. When I returned, I went straight to the Corporal in Charge. I told him they were here to protect us, not to make it necessary for protection. I said that we had never experienced an incident like this before and that even the Konkombas had always taken good care of us. I suggested that if policemen found it necessary to come to our house, there should be two, never one. I informed him that if an incident happened again, I would not go to him but to the police in Yendi. He apologized and I heard that he dealt sternly with the offender. It never happened again.

Missionary Vernon Driggers wrote us that he was bringing his son, Bradley, to visit the north before they went on furlough and they would stay in Saboba one night. They came, brought the news that the Del Mundo, the ship carrying our freight, had broken down, and was in Monrovia, Liberia for repairs! Ann gave her room to the guests and slept in our spare half-bed on the faithful old screened in porch just near the head of my bed. We talked around a doorframe far into the night. This freight palaver had given us a mutual problem to talk about! We discussed hundreds of fence posts someone had put, not just around our house and the clinic, around the entire mission property. Most posts had rotted and were on the ground. It had not been priority until our house was livable. One Tuesday in early July, Ann took the clinic while Biyimba did our wash. I drove to Yendi with Abraham and brought a load of teak fence poles to replace those fallen down. Then, as we were eating our usual Tuesday beans for lunch, we were called to treat an eight-year-old comatose girl with cerebral malaria or poison. They refused a trip to Yendi; she died the next day.

One morning in July 1969, as we met with house and clinic employees for prayer and reading of God's Word on the *palaver porch*, Dondow asked, "Do you know there is an American on the moon today?" We knew! It had waved in and out all night on our short-wave radio from Monrovia, Liberia or American Armed Forces Radio in Europe! Dundow kept shaking his head and muttering. Finally, he said, "I believer you Americans can do anything!" That reminded me of the time the corn grinder man said to Gylima and me, "White man never lies." I thought, "Americans can't do everything and some do lie, but a man on the moon!"

Our problems, for the moment, were more down to earth. In the midst of the Wednesday maternity clinic, another family brought an unconscious teenage girl with malaria. We were still treating her, and about eighty other sick people, on Friday when two men were brought in with snakebite. We treated one and observed the other, as his foot was not swollen. His blood clotted well and the wound did not look like fang marks. We dressed the foot, but sent him home with instructions of what to watch for. The rains were truly running the snakes out of the ground, and treatment was getting expensive!

With treatment, the young girl with malaria became lucid and recovered enough by Saturday that I drove her home to Toma in the VW. The people usually had ways to get their people to clinic and home on the back of a cow or in a hammock held on the shoulders of two men. I went to Toma partly because I needed to talk with Karen, Pastor Namyela's wife. He had gone to Tamale for a committee meeting so I was to speak at the church on Sunday morning. As I was leaving Toma, they brought Tiborwir Bilingan, who was in labor with her tenth child. I took her to the clinic and she delivered a five-pound girl at 11 P.M. All day Saturday Ann had been going from village to village to buy and haul the rest of the two hundred bundles of dry grass required to finish the roofing of our house. Still, when she returned, she came to help with Tiborwir's delivery!

On Tuesday, July 15, we went to Yendi to get the third load of fence posts. When we returned we found a family of four from the coast in our house. They had arrived from America recently and were being acquainted in Ghana. They spent the night. They reported that more visitors were coming the next day. While we had maternity clinic on Wednesday, nine more arrived. They took pictures as we treated the women. We fed thirteen visitors at noon with only six spoons and six forks; our freight had not come. The new missionary family left after lunch. The others were members of a mission committee. They had come to choose a location for the Turner Memorial Chapel. It was to be in memory of Virginia Turner, the American nurse killed while itinerating. She had planned to work at Saboba clinic. They decided her memorial would be built on mission property, between our house and the market, about a block from our house. The committee would handle the money and hire a contractor. We liked that, as we already had more than enough building in progress.

I had mentioned in a letter to Virginia, before I knew she was dead, how badly the nurses needed a house in Saboba. If we had combined the money I raised with what was given from the Turner family, it would have built a house for the nurses. I could not believe Virginia Turner would have been disappointed with that. The possibility was never mentioned. I certainly was not opposed to having an all-tribes church in the Saboba Market area; it was over a mile from the Toma church.

The committee members left, not knowing what our house looked like when we first got there or how hard we had worked so they could even sleep there one night. They showed no interest in our building projects. My heart fell down, but only Ann knew it. She usually did something nice for me when she knew I felt sad. When we were called to a delivery July 30, she offered to let me sleep and she delivered a baby on her own. All was normal; she got along fine and seemed pleased with her effort!

The following Saturday, while Ann went to Yankazia in the VW to have clinic, I went to Kokonzoli. I brought back several young men in the pickup to put the bundles of grass on our house. We had been stockpiling them. We paid the young men, as they had families to feed. That evening we both went to take them home. A bridge had washed out in the last rainy season and was being replaced; we had to detour through the water. We stayed late for a service at the church. As we returned home in the dark, the water was deeper. The lights were submerged for an instant and we were in total darkness; brakes are useless for a time after that.

A letter arrived from the pastors in the Bimoba Section. They invited us to come to the dedication of a new church in Najong #2. They said they postponed the dedication until I came from America so I could attend because of the rescue at Najong #2 in 1959. Rev. Namyela received an invitation for two reasons. He had also been beaten in the rescue effort and, as Northern Ghana District Superintendent, he was asked to be the main speaker at the dedication. When the day came, we drove to Nakpanduri Clinic and on to Najong #2. The nurses at Nakpanduri clinic in 1969 were Eloise Smith and Ruth Anderson. Ruby Johnson was coming out to sort through her drums in preparation for returning to America permanently. She would fill in at Nakpanduri Clinic, with a MAPS nurse, after the present nurses left. Joy King and Sharon Wallace would arrive soon from the UK, when their midwifery training was complete. Many pastors and missionaries were in Najong #2 for the dedication of the new church. When I saw it, I was jolted to remember a letter written to me from Teacher Samson Mankrom and the Chief of Yankazia immediately after the Najong #2 rescue. They predicted there would be a church built on the spot where we were injured. There it was! I could have stood at the new Najong #2 church and tossed a stone to where I fell. Many Bimobas who participated in the 1959 beating were present for the church dedication in 1969. Some smiled at me in wonder; others seemed more stern or perplexed. The Sunday School Superintendent was among those who had once beaten us. There, on the front seat, was the village chief who had held the keys to my vehicle in his hand so we could not escape. His son, Simon Dzato, was a student at Northern Ghana Bible Institute (NGBI) preparing to be a pastor. The man who ordered the kidnapping and beatings sat beside the chief. His son, John Saban, was also in NGBI preparing to be a pastor. That made four young men from Najong #2 who were either pastors or in Kumbungu preparing to be pastors. Deacon Elijah and his wife may have been the only Christian family in Najong #2 in 1959; they were beaten along with us. The young men from Najong #2 gave credit to their beloved Deacon Elijah for their going to NGBI; that number almost tripled through the years. As planned, Rev. Namyela was the main speaker for the church dedication. It was emotional for him, he had pastored in their area for years. He knew the people; some facing him had beaten him. While there, he had gone to prison for the communist religion of political correctness. About halfway through his message, he put his arm across the pulpit, laid his head on it, and wept. The situation produced deep emotion in everyone, but it was also a healing occasion. I cannot remember seeing Chief Nyankpen there. He had been my clinic helper when he was beaten; now he was chief over those same people and villages. Pastor E.J. Namyela, Ann Fisher, and I traveled back to Saboba that same day.

In the first week of August, a letter came from Eddie Ziemann. After eight months, our long lost freight had arrived in Takoradi Harbor. Eddie said there was truly no camper shell for Ann's pickup. I cannot remember that it ever came, but we kept hauling, building, and transporting sick people! Eddie concluded his letter with, "This is too wonderful! (African for, 'Full of wonder!') So goes missionary life and how we love it!" Within days, Think Twice brought our freight. I noticed that he, like me, was not so young any more. Biyimba, Abraham, and the clinic workers came to help unload. Some metal barrels with soldered lids had been broken open. One wooden crate had been impaled; Ann's damaged mattress was visible through a gaping hole. This was not surprising after long storage, a strike, and a steamer breakdown. When Think Twice left, we dug into a second set of drums. The New Mexico District Council had bought a new typewriter and given me their used one. Apparently, it had been removed, dropped, damaged, and returned to one of the drums with broken locks. I had been looking forward to a full size typewriter, or ANY typewriter. Rollers and screws were missing from the new typing table. One of the two beautiful bedspreads, provided by Mrs. James Brankle and the Las Cruces women, was missing. I could understand how tempting that could be! After waiting eight months for our freight, our reactions went from moans of woe to screeches of delight. The washing machine, sewing machine, and RV toilets arrived unscathed. The month of August was a repeat of going through Ruby's barrels so we could return them to Tamale. Our house was better to live in while we sorted, this our third time. We took the typewriter to Tamale. The repairman said, "I think this typewriter was dropped; that caused so many things *to* get bend." My diagnosis exactly! He said he would have to manufacture some parts. Hal Lehmann said he thought I was typing too fast and it rather melted.

Late in August, Ann left in her pickup to take fifteen lads, primary through middle school ages, to camp held at a Government Technical School in Tamale. As they loaded and left, I was at the clinic delivering a boy to Bingijir Kojo of Toma. That same day I treated seventy-five people in the general clinic, including two snakebites. The next day, Joel Ubor and I treated twenty-six people at Yankazia. By the time I got back to Saboba, I was forced to bed by a raging high fever and the malaise of malaria. I wondered if Ann had done the same in Tamale. I started myself on heavy Chloroquin. Pastor Namyela and our house and clinic helpers came to pray for me. The Africans knew about malaria; I felt I was in the best hospital. The following Tuesday a young girl from Zongo, the market village, had her first baby. After a difficult delivery, the baby lived only twelve hours. Before Ann returned, I had delivered a third baby, a healthy girl, for Nilemo from Buagbaan. The Ghanaian clinic helpers managed to treat the sick people within clinic hours. When Ann returned at the end of that week, she was even more exhausted than when she left. The roads were muddy and difficult to drive. She had one flat on the way to camp and one returning to Saboba. One rim was so rusted that it broke through; she caught a ride ten miles back to Tamale to have a tire mounted on the last rim we had. While Ann rested, I wrote letters. Thank God, we did have a good cook! Eventually, we took inventory of the food we brought and Ruby's food we kept. Biyimba still had his index cards with menus; we set up a rotation of menus. We still went to the storeroom daily for items he would need. Biyimba went into our storeroom at times to get kerosene for the fridge and lights. We learned that, in general, Konkombas were not thieves. There were possibly two reasons, if they were not Christians. If someone was caught stealing, a certain cry was given and the whole village went after the t'ief-man! They said if the Germans caught someone stealing, their thumbs were cut off to identify them as a thief. That should teach anyone!

One day in our mail, there was a letter from Rev. and Mrs. Raymond Hudson. I had stayed in their home for years when itinerating in New Mexico. At that time, he was District Superintendent in New Mexico, while she was Director of the Women's Ministries. He had recently taken a position in the Stewardship Department at the General Council Headquarters in Springfield, Missouri. Another letter was from my mom. She wrote that they had bought a fast food franchise in Alamogordo. I was never very surprised what they did next! I am like them.

In September, Ann and I were attempting to deliver twin girls for Amilia Apeki, wife of a local policeman. The twins seemed to be locked and neither was descending. We had been with her all the night before. We decided to transport her to Yendi, but there was flooding of both roads out of Saboba at the Yombeteu River. It runs north and south between Saboba and Wapuli, then it circles east between Saboba and

Kokonzoli and joins the Oti River. On the Wapuli road, Ann waded in to evaluate the depth of the water, but when it got above her knees, we decided against crossing. The bridge was still a city block ahead. As we waited, an African came walking through water above his waistline while carrying his bicycle above his head. We would have taken the woman across in a canoe, but the local police said there was rioting in Yendi over a chieftainship. The ambulance could have met us on the far side of the river, but it was busy transporting the injured and dead. Seems there were about forty people dead, some on mission property near the Yendi bungalow. (Anne and Becky had come from England recently and were to live in Yendi. When they got as far as Tamale, they waited there until it was safe to go on to Yendi.)

Ann Fisher and I decided to stay safely in Saboba, on the other side of Yendi! We were, however, certainly praying about the problem at hand—locked twins! We often said, "The best form of induction of labor is a trip over the road to Yendi." It worked again! We drove back to Saboba; the twin girls unlocked and were born shortly, one in a breech position. One weighed three pounds, four ounces, the other four pounds, five ounces. Two days later we delivered a boy, Isaac, for Mata and Abraham.

Abraham was our Kusasi yardman from Bawku, a town near the border between Ghana and Haute Volta (Burkina Faso). He cut wood, carried water, and kept the grass cut low in our yard so we could see snakes. Mata was a tall, willowy, beautiful, Kusasi girl who looked regal in her clothing. We watched their children grow in our yard.

A week later Ann and I drove both vehicles to Tamale because we had to take several pastors. The roads were passable but the mud was deep. The water's height between Saboba and Wapuli was lower, but there were still trucks and a tractor with lugs off the road in mud and water. We were told that some of the lorries would be there until dry season.

In Yendi, all was quiet, but airplanes were on the landing strip. Soldiers examined the content of our vehicle between Yendi and Tamale. We asked them about the airplanes. They said it was to prevent a former political personality to take advantage of the riots and attempt a takeover of Ghana by coming in a back door.

In Tamale, we ate a meal at the Government Catering Rest House for Ann's birthday. I drove back to Saboba in the VW. She left the pickup in Tamale for her return. She and the pastors had arranged rides to Kumasi to attend the West African Conference. I stayed in Saboba as I had been to a West African Conference before. I felt we had been gone from Saboba too often. If the rains isolated Saboba, I could be of some medical help. Several women had babies due. The rains triggered many pneumonia cases, especially in babies. While Pastor Namyela was gone, I spoke at the Toma Church. On Sunday morning, about four front rows of teenagers were looking toward me intently. I was delighted that they were absorbing every word! When we said the last, "Amen," they were up on the platform like a swarm of bees. They pointed behind me. A four-foot snake was going back and forth on a rafter trying to reach a bird's nest.

1. (L-R) Maternity, Snakebite, General, waiting rooms. 2. Medical officials at clinic opening 1969. 3-4. Clinic helper, Dundow, ringing emergency bell and with daughter, Helen, before and after rehab. 5-6. Twins. A policeman and our cook and family, Biyimba and Makpa. 7. (L-R) Emmanuel, Gewen, Solomon and Joel (in a study of moods). Off to nursing and theology schools. 8. Councilman Jager and his son, Tadimie helping yardman, Abraham to roof our house.

CHAPTER THREE

Four Churches Ready for Use
Helen Dondow Can Walk

WITHIN A WEEK, ANN returned with the pastors. We continued to be deeply involved in providing medical care in the area and helping pastors with their goals for the churches. There was no way the two could be mutually exclusive. Treating the sick brought grateful people into the churches. Teaching them a faith that included healing for both body and soul helped them in all of life's choices. When I applied to go as a missionary, one thing was emphasized. I was told that my nursing was a means to an end, not the end. The Mission Board required me to graduate from a Bible College and have practical experience in the Christian ministry before I left America. That policy changed by necessity, and they eventually sent new graduate nurses, without the Bible College or midwifery.

There were two specific problems that concerned all mission nurse-midwives on clinic stations in Ghana, and they were certainly known at mission headquarters. 1) The nurse-midwives needed better housing. If young nurses came to stay full time, they would be playing Russian roulette with their health, when it was unnecessary! There could have been a new house for them! What nurses did to have lodging each time they arrived in Saboba was far beyond nursing. Problems such as this were reasons why Helen and I originally asked for a clinic committee; we thought they would help. 2) The staffing of midwives was inconsistent.

The clinics at Saboba, Nakpanduri, Techamentia, and Walewale were officially registered with the Ghana Government as midwifery clinics. A mission committee allowed Ann and Becky, the two British midwives, to refuse to go to a nursing station again. They located at Yendi to work on literature. That was not nursing exclusively. They insisted it was God's will and perhaps it was because of their age. Ann and Becky knew the younger ones were coming. Hilda Palenius, Joy King, and Sharon Wallace were all in midwifery training in the UK and thought they would soon be ready for clinics in Ghana. Hilda eventually chose to go to Nigeria. With the loss of Helen to sick parents, Ruby to cancer, Hilda to Nigeria, and Becky and Ann to literature from the already inadequate pool, and gaining only Joy and Sharon, the situation was deteriorating. We suffered when we left and closed a clinic; we knew the people would suffer. We suffered with complicated cases when we were sent to where a clinic had been closed for some time. The mission clinics were remote; the Ghana Government might still never staff medical facilities there unless the mission continued to supervise it. The solution could be for the mission to accept Ghanaians trained in Ghana to keep personnel. I felt God led in my life to get me prepared in England. He had a reason; the mission pledged medical help. God saw and provided Ruby, Ozella, Becky, Anne, Helen, and me. However, there were no local schools and certainly no girls in the schools. Now there were both girls and boys that could be educated in their system and staff mission clinics. Why not utilize the available?

To some missionaries, the old Saboba house was almost a convenient icon and untouchable. It had truly been acquired by a miracle; it was held together by a miracle too! We made it livable each tour, at the expense of our health! Adequate housing would need to be provided for young American nurses to consider even coming. They could, or would never do what Ruby and I did. Some men said it would even be difficult for them. Like Becky and Ann, we older nurses would not have the strength to cope with it forever. The reality was that Ann and I had just revived the Saboba house and clinic in 1969, exactly as Helen and I had in 1954. Fifteen years with no progress, what were they thinking?

While I was in USA recovering, I persuaded people in New Mexico and Kansas to sponsor young men at both Northern and Southern Bible schools. Yes, we were nurses and doing more than nursing, as it should have been. That was getting ready for the indigenous church. It was time to change the clinic process also, but not let it die after using it to open churches. In the early '50s, we did not have Konkombas to send away to nurses training. Local schools were too new and in 1969, there were still very few girls in local school. Most girls had been bargained for at birth to be wives; any schooling for them was considered wasted efforts. The time was fast approaching to get Ghanaians trained to replace us, simply because the American midwives were not going to be available. Our suggestions about training Ghanaians were ignored or requests denied. Did they not want African nurses trained for the clinics, or did they just not want the clinics? The Konkombas say, "If you agree, your mother dies; if you disagree, your father dies. So, state your position!" That about explains the problem! If we wanted better housing for American nurses, we were in trouble; if we wanted Africans trained to replace us, we were in trouble. Each time, we returned to bad housing after suffering to find a nurse coworker, forget a midwife! It would even be good to have a doctor at Saboba Clinic! A schoolteacher in Saboba named Joseph Nteapuah Biniyam had contacted someone about medical education in the USA. I followed with letters of recommendation. Even my sister and family in San Diego said if he found a school in that area and was admitted, they could furnish a place to stay and food, but not tuition. Teacher Joseph was the son of Makambi, the little lady who died in childbirth while being transported to Tamale the week before Ann and I got there. Joseph would have been competitive even in American schools. He asked us to talk to his father, Biniyam, about the finances. The man said, wisely, that he did not have that kind of money to send his son for education and care for the rest of his family. Joseph finally got enough money for a round-trip fare, but not tuition. My sister and family were not willing to provide food and lodging for a three-month visit; they wanted to do it for his education! Again, an African proverb aptly says, "If you build a house for a man free of cost but you leave one wall out, he will hate you forever." I do not say Joseph hated us; I believe he thought we gave up too easily. I felt we tried hard. What stopped the endeavor was that no one had the money for full school tuition. That's one big order! I do not know if he ever got to be a doctor, he would have made a fine one!

Ann and I were continuously upgrading our dwelling. For example, at one point water had not run through the pipe into her bathroom for some weeks. She had been bathing in the bathroom in the main house. There we checked for snakes in a cement tub; they came up through the drain. If safe, we got in. We soaped all over and then poured a washbasin of water over us to rinse. We did this and changed clothing more than once a day when the weather was so hot. One day the mud content and tadpole count in that bath water was just too high. Abraham helped us take every pipe loose outside of both bathrooms. We found dead leaves and mud mixed with dead lizards and snakes. We made use of the packing drums used in shipping our freight. If the barrels came from road striping gangs where they already had paint inside, they didn't rust through as quickly. If items of food were stored for months in those painted barrels, because of a harbor strike and a ship's breakdown, the food could absorb paint odor. We learned all that by experience! More than nursing! Near the end of this project, Abraham said, "You know, these have not been cleaned since the ladies hired me." One morning our kerosene refrigerator was not freezing, although the fire was still burning below it. We killed the fire, removed the kerosene tank from beneath it and the food from inside it. Biyimba and Abraham turned the whole fridge upside down! We left it on its head for twenty-four hours to recirculate the gas, which caused freezing when heated. We turned it upright again, installed the kerosene tank, and lit the burner. Voila, we had ice! *More than nursing!*

Finally, Ann and I wrote home for prayer and went another route to provide for future clinic help and education for local young people completing middle school. We went to talk with directors of nursing, midwifery, and technical training facilities, mostly in Northern Ghana. We explained the problems of transportation and lack of newspapers in Saboba. The scholarships were often announced in the papers and we heard too late to help the Konkombas. We introduced them to our need of present and future nurses and midwives at the clinics. We found they would train the young men and women who passed the exams given at certain times. Then that trained nurse could come back and help us. We went back to Saboba to observe for possible candidates as we taught in the local schools. We hired the brightest and most aggressive ones to work in our clinics; we could evaluate them and discover their own future educational goals. We transported them wherever necessary for testing or admission; our efforts were not limited to medical.

One of those treks was to Tamale. There we saw results of a very bad accident. It involved a huge truck and a car that looked like the one belonging to Bonnie and Peggy. We found them in the hospital badly bruised and with lacerations, but they looked like they would survive. We teased Peggy that

she now had a Ga tribal mark! I still had mine from a wreck
in Albuquerque at age five. Soon after Ann and I returned
to Saboba, the Hal Lehmanns wrote for us to come back to
Tamale and be with Bonnie and Peggy, who had just gotten home from the hospital. Hal and Naomi needed to meet
a plane in Accra. It was bringing their daughter, Gretchen
Cast, and her Swiss husband from Lesotho, South Africa for
a visit. The Lehmanns were leaving very soon on furlough
to the USA. Gretchen was the fourteen-year-old-girl who
stayed with me for two weeks in 1957 after Helen Kopp was
forced to go to her ill mother in America. Gretchen's dad told
me not to make her into a single missionary; obviously, I
hadn't! When the Lehmanns returned to Tamale, Ann and I
went back to Saboba. Then, on an afternoon of the last week
of October, Hal and Naomi brought the Casts to visit us at
Saboba. They stayed two nights and one full day. Gretchen
knew Pastor Namyela and his wife, Karen. Together, we visited pastors and churches in the Saboba area. They taught the
Konkombas some new songs in both English and the Lesotho languages. The clinic schedule went as usual and yet we
found time to play table games and even croquet outside.
I had never gotten the septic tank put in, but the RV toilets
that arrived were self-contained and needed servicing only
once a week. With the chemicals, they had no odor; it was
definitely a step up from the sand bucket! We put a sign on
the wall above the toilet, "Pump water into bowl with handle
at right. LEAVE HANDLE DOWN. Empty bowl with lower
lever at right. Repeat if necessary, using brush." Eventually,
Hal came out to announce, "I never knew you had to have a
pilot's license to operate one of those things!"

The funeral of a very important person took place the
first week of November 1969. It was for Gaemba, Amos Biyimba's mother. The custom was that when a husband died
the wife would go to one of his brothers to be cared for or
be one of his wives. She had refused to marry after her husband died and raised her family alone. She helped all the

American nurses by sitting with maternity cases and mothers with sick babies at the clinic. Her sons that I knew were Bileti, Jager, Biyimba (our cook), Makuba, and Torba; she may have had others. When Geamba died, Pastor Namyela was one hundred eleven miles away at NGBI in Kumbungu for committee meetings involving his official capacities. We drove to Kumbungu and brought the pastor to Saboba. A body had to be buried within twelve hours; there was no embalming. After the funeral, we took the pastor back to Kumbungu; that was about eight hours of driving. Her sons had a Christian funeral, but not without challenges from the extended family. A memorial service took place at the church on Sunday morning, November 2. They sang so many songs it reminded me of my grandmother's funeral in America.

The rains had stopped over a month before and the weather was dreadfully hot in November. Cards must be mailed that month to get to New Mexico by Christmas. We got an iced drink and addressed cards to family, friends, and supporters while audiotapes played Christmas music. I had sold my army surplus wind up record player. To have a little time for us, we changed the weekly clinic schedule. Wednesday was still for the prenatal women and child welfare clinic in Saboba. We kept Monday and Friday for general clinic in Saboba. Attendance increased when we omitted general clinic on Tuesday and Thursday. On those two days, one of us stayed in Saboba for emergencies and deliveries. If these were light, we could write letters and work on lesson plans for Religious Instruction in the area schools. Schoolchildren learned it as fast as we produced it; we needed a duplicator! On Tuesday and Thursday, the other nurse went with some of our young Konkomba helpers to Kokonzoli, Sambuli, Gbenja, Wapuli, Sanguli, Yankazia, or some other village five to eleven miles from Saboba. They held child welfare clinic, passed out American surplus food when it was available, and had Religious Education where there was a Ghana Government school. At clinics involving preschool children, we routinely evaluated their weight, and gave them vitamins and prevention or treatment for malaria. We could not buy childhood immunizations. When they were available at Government Medical Stores, we gave them. At any town, in any epidemic, we helped the Ghana Government by giving five hundred to seven hundred cholera or other injections per day, which they provided.

Our clinic helper, Dondow, and his wife, Nanabikina, had a daughter, Helen, their firstborn, who was five years of age and crippled by polio. Nanabikina was the daughter of Beso Akonsi, the beloved deacon in the Toma Church. Dondow's Helen could not walk upright. She could move quickly in a sitting position as she slung her legs along. She said she wanted to walk upright like her younger sister. It so touched my heart that I dreamed one night that Helen Dondow was taken to Carrie Tingley Hospital for Crippled Children in New Mexico. It was located in Hot Springs (TorC) at the time. My dad worked in their engine room to generate electricity for wet or dry heat therapy. Carrie Tingley was the wife of New Mexico's Governor Tingley at the time the hospital was built. The building in TorC is now used for retired American veterans, because Carrie Tingley Hospital for Crippled Children was moved to Albuquerque for teaching purposes. As an instructor in nursing education, I assigned student nurses there. It was good clinical practice in pediatrics and rehabilitation. In my dream Mary Steel, the first of the two British Wycliffe translators to live in Saboba, stopped by the hospital in New Mexico and interpreted for Helen, as she could not speak English. I may have dreamed it because the two Wycliffe Marys were over for dinner one evening. In reality, after the Nalerigu doctors informed us about the Rehab Center, we wrote for an Accra missionary to investigate and make an appointment for Helen. The last week of November, we drove both vehicles to Tamale. Ann parked her pickup and she, Dondow and Helen went by plane to Accra. We did not have the money to do this, but Helen could not sit on our doorstep without help.

On my way back to Saboba, I got our mail at the Yendi Post Office. Dad wrote about the success of his deer hunt. I had always gone with him when I could. There were packages from the women in New Mexico churches. One from Mountainair had the makings of a total Mexican dinner. I knew I had to wait for Ann before eating that; West Texans love Mexican food too. Young men just out of Saboba Middle School helped me while both Ann and Dondow were gone. They were Joshua Gewen Beso, Gideon Tadimie Jagir, Solomon King Binambo, Emmanuel Gondow, and Joel Ubor Wumbei. My full-time worker, David Brown Magbaan, was a bit older; he had recently married Helen Beso, a sister to Dondow's wife. That made our two full-time clinic workers brothers-in-law. We delivered three babies after Ann left and before I became violently ill with dengue fever. Dondow returned by plane to Tamale and by market lorry on to Saboba. He brought a letter from Ann; she had become violently ill with dengue fever in Accra. The rehabilitation personnel had evaluated the strength in Helen's legs and hips. They decided to combine physical therapy, braces, and crutches to help her walk. Dondow, David and the young men were running the Saboba Clinic with only consultation from me. When a very difficult delivery, a walk-in, appeared on December 7, I knew I was too ill to care for her. I took both of us to Yendi Hospital where she eventually delivered and went home to Saboba. On the way to Yendi that day, we met Ann on her way to Saboba. She was still ill! We convinced her to return to the hospital with us. Dr. Korsah at first suspected typhoid; it was dengue fever. You think you're going to die, but very few do; even that would be from complications. We were so grateful that a fine doctor had come to Yendi and the hospital was available. This trip to Africa had been an endurance test of unpacking, packing, unpacking, and packing drums. We had one sickness right after another.

I fell twice at the clinic hard enough to injure my back. I became depressed; that was common with dengue fever. We were soon back doing the clinic work on schedule.

On December 18, we drove to Tamale for a *Top Ten* Christmas party of all single missionary ladies in Northern Ghana stations. We were back in Saboba by December 21; we all wanted to be in our area churches for Christmas celebrations. At our house, we put up a little artificial tree. On Christmas Eve, the young people presented a skit at Toma Church. That evening we went roaming (caroling) with them. Afterward they, along with our workers, and the pastor's family joined in a party at our house. We played games, popped popcorn, and drank punch. After they left, Ann and I opened our few gifts on the tree. Hal and Naomi Lehmann, Bonnie, and Peggy arrived from Tamale on Christmas day. Some went to Yankazia and churches down that road for Christmas celebrations. Some went to Kokonzoli to celebrate with that church. That evening all six of us drove to Tamale, where Ann and I slept for four days! We returned the typewriter we had borrowed from Lehmanns; they were going on furlough to America soon. We still had no typewriter.

Our little Helen Dondow was in Accra without her family for Christmas! Her family was missing her and her mom, was expecting their fourth child. We knew Helen could speak neither English nor the coastal languages. One Wycliffe translator, Mary Abbott, was due for a short furlough to England. As she was on her way out of Ghana, she did indeed go to visit five year-old Helen in Accra. Helen was so happy to speak her language. She said, "I tried Lekpakpaln, Dagbani and Hausa languages, but nobody could hear me." Mary asked, "Then what did you do?" Helen replied, "I learned their language so I could get to the bathroom." As soon as Ann and I returned to Saboba to run the clinic, Dondow went to Accra and brought Helen back to Saboba. She was walking upright with braces and crutches! Dondow said that many people asked him on the lorry, "What kind of father would take a daughter over five hundred miles, leaving his family and employment, to help his crippled child?" Even we had to start by asking at the Nalerigu Hospital. Both Dondow and Helen were so proud! She left in 1969 scooting on the floor; she returned in 1970 walking upright! She walked to our bungalow to show us she could walk upright! The hand carved wooden crutches looked so heavy and bulky, but her smile of delight is permanently etched in my mind. She started to school. At first Dondow took her to school on his bicycle before he came to the clinic to work each morning. She walked the half-mile back home after school. Within weeks, Dondow wrote this letter:

> To Madams Spencer and Fisher, a congratulatory note: I have the honor to submit here this letter thanking you for your charitable act by helping me to send my child to Accra. I don't know how much thanks I can express to make you really understand. I can only pray to God to help and strengthen you more and more. You were not able to give the kind of help you gave without God's help. So, God bless you in all you accomplished and reward you. I would not have been able to sponsor my child to Accra and back home. I would not have been able to save that much money, ever! The Bible says, 'Blessings be on those who help the needy.' I thank God for my working in the clinic so I can care for my family. I started with a scanty salary but now I earn sufficient to make me content to continue working there. God has rewarded me by giving you wisdom to help both my daughter and me. Again, may God bless you. When I first started working in the clinic, there was no water tank (cistern for collecting rainwater). I was forced to carry water on my head. Some men would have run away, saying that was women's work or too hard. I never did! I thank God for giving me the patience. Now, I have my reward! If I had not been working at the clinic, I would have had my wife and family to feed and

a crippled child. Who would have helped me to send a child to Accra? So I thank God very much and you two! God bless you always.

Ever yours, Edward Dondow

The next time I went to America and returned to Ghana from a furlough, I took Helen some lightweight metal fore-arm crutches.

On January 4, Ann and I went to Yankazia for the morning worship service and Kokonzoli in the evening where we arrived before dark. Pastor Dahamani stayed for the service in Kokonzoli, but some of his church members went with us to Sambuli for a service in the chief's compound. Ten people accepted Jesus, the crucified Son of God, as their Sacrifice by faith. Those from Kokonzoli pledged to return on foot or bicycle and teach them how to make Him the Lord of their lives. When this kind of visit took place, it probably meant that a church would be established soon.

The next morning, Pastor Namyela and I took a mason to Yankazia to plan and measure for the next church building. That church had many older men in their congregation. The chief and many had been Christians for years, but mud churches just fell down like their houses. What we met was surprising! The young men from the Kokonzoli Church had walked miles, brought the adobe frames, and were making adobe bricks for the Yankazia Church. The mason measured off for the building and we left the Christians digging for the foundation. Halfway between Yankazia and Saboba, on the talcum powder way, Pastor Lekpamba stopped us at Gbenja and said his wife, Bage, had been in labor too long. She delivered their Naomi just after midnight on the sixth. We slept a while and then Ann went for child welfare clinic in Sanguli. Three days later, we delivered Joy, another girl, for Karen Namyela and the Toma pastor. Gideon, their only son, ran to the bush and they never saw him for hours. He had five sisters and this made six. He wanted a brother so badly! Anne and Becky came from Yendi on January 18, when Naomi Lekpamba and Joy Namyela were dedicated to God. We delivered ten babies in January, in the midst of a very busy time of preliminary building. Six were girls. One boy was for Konpii of Kokonzoli. The little mother was another daughter of Beso, the beloved Toma Church deacon. (Konpii had a son who drowned in the Oti River a few years later; could this be the one?)

The Homer Goodwins went on leave to the USA. Anne and Becky moved from Yendi to Kumbungu to help teach at NGBI until the McCorkles returned from furlough. Franklin McCorkle wrote that they were bringing out a drum of supplies for us with their freight. It was from Pastor and Mrs. Orval Kiddy in Santa Fe. It would be mostly baby shirts, blankets, and bandages for the clinic. People in the New Mexico churches were truly mobilized for Ghana clinics.

☙ ☙ ☙

In the early months each year, we had to make time to go to three conferences: Northern Ghana District Council, Ghana General Council involving two Districts, and a Missionary Conference. In 1970, they combined the General Council with a ministers' seminar at Kumbungu. Hal Lehmann presented a paper on "The Minister: His Call and Commission." It was outstanding! Sometime during that General Council, E.J. Namyela, the Toma Church Pastor, was voted in as General Superintendent of the Ghana Assemblies of God. He offered to resign as Superintendent of Northern Ghana District, but the pastors did not accept it. During one of those meetings, I got my typewriter from the repairman; it never did work. With form letters, teaching in the schools, and helping Rev. Namyela write his official letters, I should have bought a new typewriter and duplicator a year ago. Thanks to thoughtful Everett Phillips at headquarters in the USA! He sent money from my surplus for a new typewriter and duplicator and asked Speed-the-Light to replace the funds later. The third conference, the Missionary Conference, was always planned for Kumasi, Takoradi, or Accra in the south in February and March. Those were the hottest months in the north. Just before we left Saboba, we delivered a boy at the clinic for Ngabil, Bileti's wife, on February 11; Bileti had been one of our very first clinic helpers years ago. We went to the conference, but were back in Saboba for clinic on Monday, February 22. We missed very few Religious Instruction classes and we were back in time for a pastors' meeting on Thursday.

〜 〜 〜

On March 2, Ann and I drove to Bawku and talked with the Matron about getting Joshua Gewen and Joel Ubor into her nursing program. She said they could go to their school and return to work at Saboba Clinic when they passed the course. On March 16, after we returned from Bawku, we delivered an eight-pound baby boy for Billijo. The women had told us our vitamins were making them have bigger babies, but they were healthier! Beso Akonsi, the beloved deacon at Toma Church, and Billijo were the parents of Joshua Gewen Beso, one of our first two student nurses from Saboba.

From March 22-29, 1970, a Good News Crusade took place in Saboba as scheduled. A platform was built in an open, grassy lot, between our house and where the Turner Church was to be built later. It was on mission property. We planned and worked hard. Young people walked to villages to inform the people while passing out literature where people could read. Literature was provided by Light-For-The-Lost, a men's organization in the churches of America. I could hardly believe a minister like Loren Fox could find time for a crusade in Saboba. I had attended his crusade in Phoenix in 1946. I suspect his coming to Saboba had a lot to do with the fact that the local Pastor Namyela was an official and heard what was available.

Rev. Fox came in a small mobile home equipped with a transformer; he could hook it up to our diesel electric generator for lights and air conditioning. We strung up lights around the platform area. Our diesel bill was high that month as March was usually the hottest month of the year. Even we who lived in Saboba were suffering. However, it was dry and the roads were passable. People came walking from many villages and even lorry loads came.

One man, who claimed to be chairman of the Saboba Town Council, wrote us a letter. He said they wanted the land the tent was on. The Mission Committee had already put in stakes where the Turner Memorial Chapel was to be built. The letter said they also wanted that land. I knew we would have to contact the Mission Committee to solve that problem, but we proceeded for the moment. That was a reminder that we were doing the work for God and not for thanks of men; newcomers were not so happy to have us.

Rev. Fox taught classes for believers at 8:30 A.M. and had evangelistic services at 7 P.M. He preached on what they must do and what Jesus could do for them. When he asked them to come with their needs, many came. Some came to accept God's Son, Jesus, as their Sacrifice so they need not sacrifice animals again. Others needed healing from illnesses, and some declared they had been healed. People came to be baptized in the Holy Spirit.

An older blind man came on the truck from Yankazia. I saw him at the altar in prayer; later, he said he tried to get up but could not. He said it seemed someone took his eyeballs out and massaged them. When they were put back, he could see; that was his testimony!

Sometimes the men of the local border patrol, even though they knew us, made us get out of the VW and lift the bonnet of our vehicle when we were coming into or leaving Saboba. One of them attended the tent meeting and came to see us the next day. He asked, "What happened to me last night? Something happened! I went home and said my rosary repeatedly until I went to sleep with my head on the table. I awoke later with extreme joy!" We explained it was God's Spirit working in him and we called it, "being born again." We read it to him from the Bible in the Book of John. He went away, but returned with the veterinarian who had been ill; his sickness left him when he went for prayer!

I believe that Gretchen Biyimba and Helen Dondow, two young girls who suffered because of polio, claimed their healing as they were prayed for. The young people used our garage as a prayer room. Some young people claimed that God had called them to be pastors, evangelists, or to some other work. One was David Mankrom Nabegmado. Many received their heavenly language as the Holy Spirit baptized them with power to overcome the evil one. I have heard the devil does not understand the language that God gives you, so he cannot intercept your requests made unto God. That is why, if you have a desperate need, you should pray in your heavenly language. Your language comes by heartfelt worship!

∿∿∿

In 1954-57, Helen Kopp and I had helped Binimpom Mankrom, a woman from Yankazia, save the life of an infant boy named David. In 1979, Ann and I found that same boy attending Saboba Middle School. He was from Yankazia, sixteen miles away, so he boarded in Saboba. The Ghana Government Schools had put Religious Instruction in their curriculum. Students and parents could choose which class in religion they would attend. David chose the class which I taught, and attended Toma Church on Sunday. One Sunday morning after the Good News Crusade and after a morning service at the church, David and Emmanuel, both from Yankazia, approached me. David said, "We want to talk to you; we want to quit middle school." "Why?" I gasped. I was shocked! They were good students; both were very intelligent and delightful. "Well," David said, "God has called us to preach; we are wasting time. We want to go to Bible School." I reminded them that the Bible School might not admit them unless they completed middle school. He sent in his application to the Northern Ghana Bible School at Kumbungu.

For a time after finishing middle school, David stayed in Yankazia. He helped us treat the people when we went there for clinic on Saturdays. When we felt he was ready, we left a skeleton of medications for him to give in our absence. We were grateful; Chief Jayum and his people were grateful. David saved lives. Emmanuel Gondow Wumbei, the other young man, completed middle school and came to work with us at the Saboba clinic. He and Joel Ubor Wumbei, one of our clinic workers who wanted to go for nurse's training in Bawku, were brothers. Solomon King Binambo was another from Yankazia area who helped us at Saboba Clinic. I remember Solomon's father so well and their faces just beamed when they were together.

Kofi, the contractor and his construction crew from Southern Ghana, came north. They had put up the new church in Yendi before coming to Saboba. When the Missionary Chairman arrived in Saboba along with a huge lorry load of lumber, cement, and other building supplies, Kofi also came to Saboba. He planned to go back and complete the interior of the Yendi church when the rains got heavy and they could not work outside on Turner Chapel. The load of building material was unloaded into our garage. It had been full of Ruby's drums and then our freight. It was a prayer room during the crusade and now it stored building material; our vehicles were never in it! When the load of building material arrived, Kofi's helpers worked so hard that we lined them up and gave them two Anacins and a multi-vite. Others also got in on the freebees. The pills became a morning ritual, as Kofi said he learned that bodies without pain and with nutrition worked harder and happier. Kofi and some of his workers joined in prayer with our house and clinic workers each morning on the palaver porch.

In early April, Kofi measured for the foundation of the Turner Memorial Chapel and men started digging. Other men were making bricks. Young girls from the Toma Church were carrying sacks of cement, almost as big as themselves, on their heads from our garage to the building site about a city block away. Local women, many from Toma Church, carried mixed concrete for the foundation on their heads in pans resembling dishpans. Sometimes the whole town looked like an anthill. Kofi was paying local people to help him with the Turner project.

Since Ann's Beautiful Blue was the only vehicle available for hauling, she or I hauled load after load of water and river sand. We had young people riding with us to load and unload. Because of this, I had to deliver many babies without Ann. She did many clinics without me. We were spreading our time so thin. Then I made a contract with Kofi to complete the projects at Kokonzoli, Yankazia, Gbenja, and Toma. We had been hauling water, sand, and cement for months. The Konkombas had been making blocks and were at different levels in the building process as labor was volunteered. Kofi wasted no time; he worked on those other churches any time he had to wait in the Turner project. We wrote and requested that Sunday school rooms be added to the plans for Turner Chapel. The request was approved and the name was changed to Turner Memorial Church. Kofi's job had grown!

We were kept busy running between Saboba and Tamale for lumber, cement, nails, hinges, and louver glass for windows. We hauled it or hired a lorry to haul it the one hundred miles from Tamale to Saboba. Then we hauled it from Saboba to Kokonzoli, Yankazia, or Gbenja. Ann got brave; she delivered babies with Dondow when I went as far as

Tamale. On one of these trips to Tamale, I reported to the Mission Committee that a man in Saboba was trying to claim the land was not ours. I had written before, but a Ghana government official came to Saboba from Yendi. Perhaps they just needed to know we were building on property truly owned by the A/G Mission.

❧ ❧ ❧

On May 3, my birthday, I delivered a girl for Nanabikina Dondow, the wife of our head clinic helper. They had girls named Helen and Janet and a boy, Paul. They named this one Mary. His children were all named for Helen Kopp's siblings. On May 16, we delivered *undiagnosed* twin boys, Peter and Phillip, for Makpa Biyimba, the wife of our trusty cook, Amos Biyimba. His first child was Ruth; the second was Gretchen. She was crippled by polio. She slung one leg as she walked, but was always busy like her father. Hannah, the next girl, was always teasing us at the clinic. She said if no one wanted a baby when it was born to call her; she wanted it! Nathaniel, Comfort, and Thomas were the youngest three until the twins came. When their mother had twins, Hannah had her baby! She carried one twin on her back while her mother, Makpa, carried the other. I cannot remember seeing Hannah without that twin; I suspect her mother was grateful for the help!

❧ ❧ ❧

The rains were late starting in 1970, and they were preceded by violent, gusty winds and dust. Saboba seldom had tornados like in Kansas, but had gusts with hurricane force. One day Kofi decided to put the roof on the Turner Church so they could work under it if the rains became heavy. The trusses were made on the ground and it took every man available to help raise them. They had nailed a few aluminum sheets on when a violent storm hit! Kofi's workers ran to their lodging. The wind blew the aluminum sheets off the church building where they had been working and some landed on the house where Kofi and his workers lived. I watched this through a window at our house. I wondered what the odds were of this happening; it was indeed *wonderful*! (Full of wonder!) No one was injured, but Kofi said he almost lost his entire crew; they wanted to run south to the coast. Contractor Kofi was a stable Christian; he even blessed the local churches. By the time everything was built, the rains were so heavy that we had to use the beautiful structures before dedication, especially Kokonzoli and Yankazia. Within the period of April through June, Kofi and his crew from the south completed work on the four Konkomba churches, except they all needed benches.

Ann and I were exhausted! We left on the first real vacation we had for at least a year. We spent only one night in cool Kumasi. Missionaries Eddie and Bernice Ziemann had gone on furlough from Takoradi and returned a year later to Kumasi. The Paramount Ashanti Chief had just died. The local papers were full of the news; they reported that he could not be buried until the sub-chiefs supplied five hundred heads to bury with him. No one would go outside alone, even in the daytime. The churches held services at 5 P.M. so everyone could be home by dark. It was said that strangers and travelers, who would not be missed soon, were in danger. Amos Biyimba usually traveled with us; we told him not to go anywhere without informing us. No one took a taxi.

We drove on to Accra, visited, shopped, and bought meds for the clinic. We ate lunch with The Honorable Mr. Yarney, the Member of Parliament for the area that included Saboba. We discussed medical school for the teacher and another young man from Zango village. We visited the American Embassy and US Information Service. We ate out at the Ambassador Hotel with the Stroud family from Southern Ghana Bible Institute at Saltpond. One day we ate at a Chinese restaurant. Great! We saw the Bob Cobbs off on their furlough by plane; they had met us when we came in. We met the Eric Johnsons at Takoradi; they came when Ziemanns went on furlough. We drove back to Kumasi on our way home. We stayed five days in the Kumasi guesthouse and ate with the Ziemanns. They took us once to the Cabin for a meal and twice to the Chicken Box, new places to eat. The University of Science and Technology was having its display of art, pottery, and sculpture. Students had already received grades so their work was for sale. We bought vases, paintings, and a water pitcher with mugs. We visited the Kumasi zoo and saw critters I had seen in the wild. Our two weeks were up and it was nearing July. We went back to Saboba to our three tin-can dinners; they really weren't so bad. It was good to be home!

We were brought back to reality by hearing three major Saboba palavers. We learned that Mary Abbot came to the rescue at the clinic on June 18. Helen Beso Magbaan, the wife of one of our clinic workers, had delivered their first baby and the placenta was retained. Dondow and Mary Abbot had her transported to Yendi for the removal. The second palaver was that the Saboba Middle School students were in shock. A very special student, Mpompii (Happiness), who went to the Toma church, had been killed. He fell from a lorry on a road near the church; the lorry ran over him. What a waste of potential! The third big palaver required more than just information on the palaver porch; it required action. Pastor Namyela, Amos Biyimba, and his brother, Bileti, came. The story they told was unbelievable! Bileti's sixteen-year-old daughter, Yajoningan, had been taken by force while we were gone. Deja vu! His firstborn child kidnapped! How could this be happening again? Rev. Namyela had been through this with me before at Nakpanduri!

While we thought about the last situation, we drove up the back Gushiago moto'way to Nakpanduri to celebrate the Forth of July with Ruby Johnson and her coworker, Barbara Liddle. We wanted to thank Ruby personally for the use of the items in her drums. Ann talked with Barbara Liddle about helping in a girls' camp in Saboba. Addie and Polly came down from Bawku for the day. Joy and Sharon were still in the UK; they would come near the end of the year to be stationed at Nakpanduri Clinic. On the way back to Saboba, I shot seven rabbits and a python. I gave the rabbits to the Ghanaians and had the python skin tanned to keep. When we got home, the diesel engine sparked but not a light came on at residence or clinic. We got out the ol' faithful kerosene lamps. The next day, I waxed brave and removed the brushes from the generator, sanded them down and replaced them. The lights came on, brightly as ever. To bring repairmen from Tamale was getting expensive. I had watched them and decided, "I can do that!" I tried and it worked. We had a bigger problem to face ahead!

1. Konkomba Section pastors: Dahamani Dagomba, Abarika Nanumba, Elijah J. Namyela Mamprusi, Lekpamba Konkomba. 2. Church repair and new sign for Gbenja. 3. Dry season road. 4-9. Process of building; all work. 10. Dedication of Turner Memorial. Contractor Kofi Mensah and crew; Sunday school rooms. Dist. Supt Gen. Supt. Namyela congratulates Turner Pastor Simon Asore. 11. Wet season road. Dedication of new Kokonzoli Church.

CHAPTER FOUR

Upii Weh! (This Woman!)
Another Kidnapping and Rescue

BILETI WAS A CHARTER member of the Toma Church; he dressed tropical ulcers at the clinic for years. His wife, Ngabel, walked with a cane. They raised their children on the front seat of that church. My fondest memories include seeing him bring his children to church, one on the back and one on the front of his bicycle, as soon as they were big enough to hold on. However, Yajoningan, his first child, had been traded to a non-Christian village when she was born. Her name means "Hold to what is right." Bileti had tried to pay money, work, or palaver (negotiate) out of an agreement he had made before he took Christ as Lord of his life. The people refused to talk; they wanted the tall teenage beauty.

With the father, mother, daughter, and Pastor Namyela begging them, they backed up a lorry to her home and forced the girl into it. She was to be the third wife of a man who knew nothing of her life in Christ. The local police feared the Konkombas, so they referred the case to the local chief. Of course, the chief ruled that since the deal was made when the girl was born, the father had no right to her.

94

When Ann and I returned from our leave at the coast, I went to talk politely to the head policeman in Saboba. He told me there was no Ghana law to free the girl. He was too late to tell me that! *Been there, done that!* I said, "You know and I know that Ghana laws protect the girl; she has a choice. If she does not want to be there, we must see that she is not forced to stay." Without stating so, he let me know I had his permission to go to his superiors in Yendi. He was living among those Konkombas he feared! With that, I left. We were praying the girl could escape and run away, but we did go talk to the Yendi police. Yes, we had a problem, but Yajoningan had a bigger one! Word came that she was afraid they would use drugs to make her willing to go to the old man so she was refusing food. Her parents felt we must free her or she would die.

On July 10, Ann was busy hauling sand and water for the building program. Dundow and I were delivering a baby boy for Piger, from Toma area. Njonabi, her husband, was our yardman back in 1955. Their firstborn, Dorcas, had grown up in our yard. After the delivery, Pastor Namyela, Ann, and I drove to Tamale to ask advice about helping Yajoningan. One man said he tended to leave it to the Africans to solve their own problems. I wondered why we should bother to give God's Word to the people, but not help them make it work. It seems love would make us help them!

A more pragmatic missionary said he would get help from a Ghanaian solicitor (lawyer). We went! The lawyer agreed with us; Yajoningan should not be left to die. He said he would come to Yendi when the court case came up and support the police who had to make the decisions. On our way back to Saboba, we reported this to the Yendi ASP (Head Policeman). All missionaries were busy and wearing as many hats as we were, so we were on our own. The next morning we were called to the Saboba Police Station. The policeman I had recently talked with had suffered a gastric hemorrhage; there was a pool of blood. Ann ran to get ice from our fridge and we stopped the hemorrhage. He was near enough to the only fridge in the Konkomba Tribe to save his life; we could have still been in Tamale! He was verbal with his gratitude.

One day, Pastor Namyela went with us to the Yendi Police Station to see how the rescue of Yajoningan was proceeding. The ASP said he would dispatch two policemen on a market lorry to find the girl if Rev. Namyela would go with them to identify her; the pastor agreed to go. The girl had been gone almost a month; she may have decided nobody cared. Pastor E.J. Namyela and I were both having flashbacks of rescuing a girl in another tribe ten years earlier. Pastor was willing to go again, although he was not from either girl's tribe. He had a pastor's heart! Ann and I returned to the clinic; babies came, snakes struck, and malaria burned. We alerted the Toma Church that Pastor Namyela needed God's help; they went to prayer.

One early morning, July 25, five of Bileti's relatives came to our palaver porch. I knew some of them quite well; some carried small sticks. They said they had heard that the Mosiman pastor (foreigner) and we nurses were asking the Yendi Police to help the girl. (The Mosi Tribe is in Upper Volta, now Burkina Faso.) Rev. Namyela was no foreigner; he was of the Mamprusi Tribe in Ghana but NOT a Konkomba. I replied, "Yes, we want to find out if the girl wants to be there. I do not believe in slavery in America or in Africa. The Ghana Government provides freedom for girls to choose whom they marry."

They said they were going to find that Mosi-man and kill him and we would see another Najong. They showed us a letter and said it was from the Yendi Police. I could not believe a policeman would inform them! Even as we spoke, a messenger came to our fence and Biyimba went to greet her. He came back saying that men had already been sent to kill Rev. Namyela.

On Saturday, we had no scheduled clinic, so we packed a suitcase. We had no idea how long we would be gone. We called Dundow to advise him about the clinic in our absence. We killed the fridge, left Amos Biyimba in charge of our house, and quickly drove the forty miles to Yendi Police Station. We saw men from Saboba on a street. We reported that to the Yendi police and they arrested them. We asked if there were Konkombas on the Yendi police force, there was one. I had known him from his Saboba Primary School years. We went to talk with him. He had written the letter because his wife was from the village that kidnapped the girl. He feared that if we got the girl back, the villagers would take his wife in revenge. He had a valid concern! We asked him, "Do you not think we would fight as hard for your wife as for Yajoningan, if your wife wanted to be with you?" He never troubled us again.

The police put us in a house to protect us for the night. We did not feel comfortable involving other missionaries and felt we should do as the police advised. We had no idea whether they found all the men who were on their way to kill the Mosi-man. We were concerned for Pastor Namyela's safety!

Local missionaries saw our car at the police station late that night and came to ask why we were still there. We went home with them; they sent for the local pastor to help us pray! Sometime after midnight a runner came to inform us that the two Yendi policemen had returned with the girl; she was in protective custody. Pastor Namyela was at the local Pastor's house. The men who kidnapped Yajoningan were in custody. The police had not taken Rev. Namyela into the village where the girl was being held. They left him at a local police station to identify the girl when they returned with her.

The Yendi Police Court presented the case quickly; Ann and I were there only three days. The Ghanaian lawyer came from Tamale as promised. We found ourselves face to face with the kidnappers as well as the uncles who had come to threaten us and kill the pastor. Bileti and his daughter were there with Pastor Namyela. The first time Yajoningan saw us she smiled as if to say, "I knew you'd come!" She looked so ill; I wanted to cry. It was not a pleasant time! The police in charge asked the girl whether she wanted that man as her husband. Without hesitation, she said, "No!" She jerked off a headscarf and said, "They shaved my head." It was bald!

The policeman asked the kidnapper why he wanted the girl when she did not want him. He replied that she would learn to love him. The ASP asked, "Why did you shave her head?" He replied, "Well, she would not eat and she kept running away; we thought her head was spoiled." The lawyer from Tamale added his only contribution, "There is no way under Ghana's law this girl can be forced to go to a man she does not want to marry." The policeman added, "We are sending the girl back with her father. This pastor and the nurses are going back to Saboba. If anything happens to them, we will hold you responsible. It does not matter who does it; you will be charged with breaking the law. You had better go back to Saboba and look after them carefully. See that nothing happens!"

The kidnappers went south to their village. Bileti, his daughter, Pastor Namyela, and the uncles who wanted to kill the Mosi-man pastor went back to Saboba on the same market lorry. This was the same pastor who had once been imprisoned for political incorrectness, the communist Ten Commandments! People who might think Rev. Namyela rushed in where angels feared to tread, must think again! He was elected General Superintendent of his church organization for sixteen years after one of the two rescues and the imprisonment. He practiced what he preached!

~ ~ ~

Ann and I went to Tamale to shop and to rest a little. Within a few days, we returned to Saboba and the clinic. One day, the Yendi Police came the forty miles to greet us and introduce the new head policeman for Saboba. He came to see us several times and we felt safe. The policeman who allowed the girl to be taken was transferred to another town; perhaps he requested it.

Once I was walking on a street in Tamale when a Ghanaian woman stopped me. She reminded me that she was the wife of the policeman who had hemorrhaged in Saboba. She said they moved to a village south of Tamale where he bled again and called for treatment by a fetish priest. Her husband had not survived; she was a widow. I hugged her and we cried together on a Tamale street.

After a few weeks in Saboba, we made another trip to Tamale with Bileti and his entourage. He presented gifts, including a chicken, yams, and other items from the girl and her family to the Tamale Lawyer for his help and support to the Yendi Police. He seemed so pleased that they had made the effort; that's all the pay he ever got!

⸾ ⸾ ⸾

The area work continued and the building projects advanced. Ann planned a girls' camp in Saboba for the first week in September. The teenage girls in Yendi area were invited. There was to be a boys' camp in Tamale the second week in September. Teenagers were cutting grass with their cutlasses from the Turner Church, near the market, to our house and on to the clinic. Our property always looked beautiful just before youth camps. We paid them by the hour, but they got no money. We kept a record of their time and money; it was used to pay for petrol or a driver and vehicle to get them to camp. The rest was for camp fees and spending money. Young people brought back such good reports that they were willing to cut grass again the next year. Pastor Namyela was planning a DVBS at Toma Church for the youngsters. A list for water baptism was growing; a new converts' course was required for candidates. Pastoring the Toma Church was no small job and he had two other demanding jobs. The early church could not afford a secretarial allowance from either District or General Council funds yet, so Ann and I continued to help with typing and duplication.

Ann was so busy with plans for the girls' camp, that I offered go bring her speaker, Barbara Liddle, from Tamale. We had met her helping Ruby Johnson at Nakpanduri Clinic. Ruby was now sorting through her drums we returned to Tamale. Midwives Joy King and Sharon Wallace had arrived in Ghana from the UK and were due at Nakpanduri Clinic any day. Joel Ubor rode with me to Tamale. At the Yambeteu River, between Saboba and Wapuli, the water covered the approach to the bridge. We planned our strategy and made it across! In Tamale, we visited Samson and Tani Mankrom and their children. Samson had been one of the first schoolteachers in Saboba in the early '50s. Now he was teaching in Tamale. One of his daughters had just completed middle school and wanted to go to the Ghana School of Community Health. I talked with the matron of the school about admitting her. Samson said he heard the church in his hometown of Yankazia was going up and beautiful. My lorry-mate, Joel Ubor, was from that area and reported firsthand. Samson sent greetings to them and said that when the parsonage was built, he was prepared to help financially. He was the teacher who wrote me a letter rightly predicting, along with U Na Febor (Chief) of Yankazia, where a Najong #2 church would be built.

We found Barbara Liddle ready to go. On our return trip to Saboba, the water over the southwest approach to the bridge was deeper and night was near. We stopped, talked, and planned. There were trucks stranded on each side with water up over the hoods; the road had to be between them. I asked Joel and Barbara to lay their hands on the dashboard of the pickup and pray. They prayed as I drove into the water. We had to get through; Ann was in Saboba alone with clinics and the girls' camp near. For a time the water rushed up over the lights and hood. We were in total darkness as the pickup dipped down, then up and sputtered to a stop on solid ground. I never shook so hard in my life! We raised the hood and allowed the engine to dry. There was water over the bridge ahead, but the railings could be seen on each side. We drove between those and on to Saboba. Barbara was young and arrived in Saboba near her birthday; she would be with us for some time. She was quickly in demand by pastors in all churches because of her artistic talent and teaching.

One morning I was treating the people at the clinic. Ann sent a note from the house, "Amos Biyimba and I baked a cake for Barb's birthday. Shall we have some for lunch or wait until the party? Signed: Fiszilhahn." Some of the Konkomba youngsters, who adored Ann, tried to say Fisher Ann instead of Ann Fisher. Their R and L can interchange, so that is how it came out. Ann loved it! We quickly set aside Tuesday evenings as a social time for the three of us.

Of course, there was no TV and only a shortwave radio that truly waved in and out. We enjoyed a lot of audiotaped music, played table games like Yahtzee, and even made up our own activities. One evening someone said, "Happiness is . . ." We all joined in to name things that made us happy or secure: a flashlight, a mosquito net, a friend to kill bugs, boiled drinking water, *any* drinking water, seeing a snake before he gets too close, a night without a delivery, a lorry mate in September rains, drums full of fuel in the rainy season, a bridge in your rear view mirror (you had made it; it was still there), Kofi the contractor, a fence around our fish bowl house, getting to travel when you plan, a lizard running on the patio when something just fell on your head from the grass roof (it could have been a snake), a new church completed, and a first rain to settle the doke. If smoke and fog is smog, then dust and smoke must be doke; we coined that long ago.

☙ ☙ ☙

After the girls' camp ended on Saturday, September 12, Ann took the Yendi girls home and ten boys on to Tamale for the boys' camp, all in one trip. She got safely over the bridge just before the village of Wapuli, dropped the girls off in Yendi and took the youths to their camp in Tamale. She left Tamale on Sunday in time to get to Saboba before dark. The dreaded river was up near Wapuli so no one could cross. Ann wrote me a note and sent it by a lad on a bicycle, "I'll return 30 miles to sleep in Yendi." She was only about ten miles from Saboba. After dark, I heard a knock on my door and I gasped! *Africans do not knock;* they clap their hands! From the note I received, Ann was sleeping in Yendi! *Then, who was at my door?* I called; Ann answered! It seems that Issaka Timbila's big mail-market lorry arrived at the water and a lugged tractor helped him get through the water. Ann parked her pickup and joined Issaka's market lorry to Saboba. Like the gentleman he was, Yakubu Timbila, Issaka's brother, walked Ann to our door. Yakubu was the second baby born at the Saboba clinic when Ruby Johnson and Ozella Reed opened it in 1949. He was now a local teacher and a freind to teacher Joseph Nteapuah Biniyam. Nteapuah (my "father's strength" or "pride-and-joy") was the son of the woman who carried her pregnancies through an umbilical hernia and died while being transported to Tamale Hospital the week before Ann and I arrived. Both Yakubu and Nteapuah wanted to go to medical school, one to Nigeria and the other to the USA; they were prime candidates.

The rains got heavier! The local police called for food to be brought in by helicopter. They asked if we had food; we did. In those cool days and nights, babies got pneumonia. We gave them little shirts from America. On September 21, we delivered a first baby, a boy, for Mary Adam, the daughter of Gylima, our first clinic helper. We were delivering babies of the second generation since Ruby and Ozella first came to Saboba.

When the mail finally did get through to us, we had a stack. My first nephew, James Michael Lynch, had married Donna McFadden in September. That triggered memories of the kiss through the bus window in Norfolk, the sacrifice of his wind-up record player, and his appointment to the Naval Academy. A letter from my long-time friend, Betty Olsen, said her sister Ruth, the "fur-lined boots lady" in New York, got married. Our stay in Africa was over half-gone. We numbered a calendar backwards to December 1971; there were four hundred sixty-five days remaining. That was a sure sign of nostalgia; it was near Ann's birthday! Word came that Eloise Smith had agreed to come to Saboba when we left, but she had no coworker yet. Joy and Sharon would still be at Nakpanduri Clinic then.

Ann and I were not the only ones missing home! The first of our clinic workers to leave and enroll in higher education was Gideon Tadimie Jagir, our language teacher. He wrote from the Teachers' College in Tamale, "I heard you and Joel were in Tamale. Every minute I looked for you, but hours passed and I lost hope you would come. Thank you for the devotional books. My friend from Saboba, Jakpir Y. Joshua, and I, are setting examples to our friends by our behavior and by having daily devotion time." He added a language lesson, "A ni Madam bee Likpakpaln do aa? N dak kee ni bee do aa. N ban kee a ni Madam gme mi Likpakpaln agbang. Uwumbor tir ni mi, Ami. G. J. Tadimie." Roughly, "Greetings; how are you and are you speaking Likpakpaln in your home? Send more devotional books."

Pastor Lekpamba Konkomba at Gbenja was a relative of Madja and Mabo's family in Nalongni, just west of the Toma Church. He wrote that he had been in Gbenja for three years and God had blessed him, but he had lost a child and was depressed. We went to be with him in services as much as we could, but our time was constantly spread so thin. It seemed that when we went to Yankazia and dropped someone off at Gbenja to be in service there, it was Ann. I believe she made that happen as she did in other cases where people were sad. She just did that; her radar was tuned to people whose *hearts fell down.*

✑ ✑ ✑

In October 1970, a letter came from young John Kitinyaab's ill father, Nampoah. Someone wrote for him. Because of his bad leg, we had driven over twenty miles to treat him in his village of Natugu, about five miles north of Wapuli. He said:

> When I was attacked by my sickness, which is still worrying me, you did your best to help. You helped my son, John, to go to youth camp by letting him cut grass. I had no money to cure my leg, how much more to afford giving him money for camp. We say the one who carries a heavy load is the one to receive your help. In fact, I have nothing more to say (I am speechless!), but I have given all the thanks to God. I had some cedis to get my son into technical school in Kumasi. You have helped with the transportation. Pray hard for my son to put his mind on what he came to do there and *put God in front.* Thank you very much.

> Your beloved man, Nampoah, John's father

The Institute of Planning and Technology (IPT) was near Kumasi, on the Sunyani road near Ayeduase. When we took John to his school, we met another Konkomba student already there, Peter Kwaku Kpolou. He was from Ehiamomkyene (Twi for *salt*), a town in the Volta Region near Chinderi and the Volta Lake. John Kitinyaab Nampoah wrote from IPT:

We plan to attend the Scripture Union together, as you advised us to join with other Christians who read God's Word. Peter and I prefer the Central Assembly in Kumasi, which is a four-mile walk. We are being advised to leave the Assembly of God. Do not let it worry you. If they force us to leave the school because of our faith, I am ready to do so. Where there are two or three gathered in His name . . . Just pray for us to get the patience of Job and the wisdom of Solomon! Greet Ann Fisher and Barbara Liddle.

John K. Nampoah

Peter Kwaku Kpolou also wrote:

The bus fee to Kumasi Central Assembly is eight pesewa in and out. We do not have that much money. - -You are now three madams in number, but I have no three stamps to write three letters. John told me about the youth camp; I pray I can go next year. John and I are living happily as Children of God. Greet Phillip Wumbei, Dewey Charles, and all A/G members.

The Matron of the Bawku Hospital Nursing School was a member of the Basil Mission of Switzerland. She kindly agreed to train two young men, Joshua Gewen Beso and Joel Ubor Wumbei, in nursing so they could return to help Assemblies of God clinics. We would be responsible for little more than transportation. The two young men from our clinic received their letters of acceptance. Their letters of thanks were so well written that we were sure we had picked the right young men to go for nurse's training in Bawku. We missed them at the clinic, but other young men filled the vacancy.

ಌ ಌ ಌ

At general clinic on Thanksgiving Day, November 26, we gave five hundred free cholera shots; that included all students from the Catholic Technical School. Then we ate turkey dinner with their staff, a European priest, a young British worker, and an American, Brother John. On Friday, Ann and I treated fifty-five patients at the clinic while Barbara was teaching at a middle school. Then we three drove to Kumbungu for the graduation of four young men at Northern Ghana Bible Institute. There were no Konkombas in that graduating class, but rather some from the Bimoba Section. They were Andrew Yambil Mbiri of Gilik and Issifu A. Kpadago of Boya. I met two from Najong #2, John Saban Yajen, and Simon Jato Masak. They would graduate in 1971. They had been in primary or middle school when I left Nakpanduri Clinic in 1960. We gave cholera immunizations to all NGBI teachers and students. Before we returned to Saboba on Saturday, we visited Gideon Tadimie Jagir at the Pupil Teachers' Center in Tamale. He said he preferred to go to nursing school. We helped him be transferred to Tamale General Hospital for their nursing program. We shopped in Tamale and drove to Saboba. The smoke from burning grass was mixing with the dust of the harmattan winds from the Sahara Desert and making it difficult to breathe.

The Ghana Information Service heard about the progress in Saboba Area. Their representatives arrived on a Wednesday after we had already treated the maternity clients that morning. Within weeks, a nice article ran in a Ghana newspaper. It said the men in Ghana Government are concerned about people in rural areas, but not able to reach all. They are grateful when needs of the people in those areas are met by missions. The article read:

> Miss E. Charlese Spencer and Miss Ann Fisher, the two nursing sisters in charge of the clinic, are also midwives. They are assisted in the clinic by two ward-assistants, a clerk, and a maintenance man. Part-time employees help with child welfare clinics in the outlying villages. The salaries of all these come from the Assemblies of God Mission. The nurse practitioners are under the direction

of the Medical Officer of Health with resident in Yendi. About fifty to seventy-five patients visit the clinic daily. Clinics in surrounding villages bring the total treated per month to over one thousand. The most common ailments treated are fever from malaria, upper respiratory infections, and skin ulcers from protein deficiencies. Skin ulcers have decreased over twenty-five percent from health teaching, improved nutrition, and a government program to eradicate yaws that the nurses co-operated in. Treatment of one thousand leprosy patients per month from Demon to Chereponi was done by Saboba clinic at one time. The Ghana Government now has a program for leprosy treatment. The Mission provides almost all the drugs except certain immunizations like cholera and childhood immunizations, the most expensive treatment being anti-venom serum for snakebites. They treat an average of five snakebites per month, with the maximum being five in a week. In November 1970, they co-operated with a government program by giving over two thousand cholera immunization injections. Since the establishment of the Saboba centre, more than two hundred forty thousand patients have visited it. Paul Konkomba was the first baby born in the Saboba maternity clinic November 3, 1949. He now works with the Ghana Broadcasting Corporation in Accra. The second baby born there was Yakubu Timbila, who hopes to be accepted for training as a medical doctor this year in Nigeria. Nearly two thousand babies have been delivered at the clinic since 1949. Three young men and one young girl are now in nurse's training programs and are expected to return to assist in the Saboba clinic and area.

Sammy Kay Edgar

The first week in December, David Magbaan and I went on Thursday, instead of Saturday, for clinic at Yankazia. We had to be sure David Mankrom had medications while we were gone. We took Chloroquin, aspirin, baby vitamins, and cough syrup. Upper respiratory problems plagued babies during the hot days and cold nights of the harmattan. During NGBI graduation, we had learned that we were required to go to West African Advanced School of Theology graduation in Lome, Togo. They were going to dedicate a new building and name it for Everett L. Phillips, Mission Secretary for all of Africa. French Togo was just two miles east of Saboba, across the Oti River, but the capitol was Lome, four hundred miles south at the coast. Pastor Namyela would go with us. On the morning of December 4, the four of us drove straight south, through the Volta Region of Ghana, to Accra. Our usual, three-day route was through Tamale and Kumasi. We crossed one arm of the Volta Lake on a small ferry and stopped to see the Akosombo dam lit up with its own electricity. We crossed a massive extension bridge into Accra. Rev. Namyela stayed with a local pastor and we stayed overnight with Jim, Delta, and young Benny Kessler. Annette was home from boarding school for Christmas; her big sister, Vangie, was in school in America. The Kesslers had moved from Tema into Accra, when the Cobb family went on furlough.

I had the VW serviced in Accra. International car registration and drivers license were required; we got those. Jim Kessler had gotten visas for all. We drove east along the coast and crossed into Togo. The big problem would be to find the home of R.C. Cunningham after dark, so we hurried. Classes at WAAST (CSTAO in French) were taught in both English and French. Students from English-speaking Ghana learned French by proximity. The next day was busy with graduation exercises and the dedication of the building to honor Rev. Phillips. His wife, Dorothy, had come from America with him. We drove back to Accra with many other vehicles from Ghana. We traveled to Kumasi the next day, spent the night, and drove on to Tamale by way of the Kintampo Road. We spent a night in Tamale, where we visited Tadimie at his school of nursing, or else we would have heard from him. We were home in exactly one week!

We arrived in Saboba to find that Sister Sophie Blocker, Matron of the Bawku Hospital School of Nursing, had come in our absence. We were embarrassed, as we were supposed to have known she was coming. The sudden trip to Lome made us forget. How could we? We wrote a letter and said we would go to Bawku as soon as possible. When we tried to wash the red dust out of our traveling clothes, Ruby's washing machine would not work. I got out the instructions for my new machine and assembled it!

In the stacks of mail awaiting the three of us were letters from both Joshua Gewen and Joel Ubor from Bawku Hospital. Gewen wrote:

> Thank you for your help in getting me started in Bawku. Our classes started November 23. Pastor Yamdogo found one room for the two of us to sleep. We have met new friends and some old—Ben, Azari, Mark, and Dickson (from youth camp) who were happy to see us. We had to report to the matron of the school at 3 p.m. She said she would write you and planned to visit you. We will receive a monthly government allowance. It was Emmanuel, Joel's brother, who wrote that you left for Lome, Togo for a graduation and dedication at WAAST. He also told us that the rains destroyed the Wapuli road. We hope to be in Saboba for Christmas; we have nine days off. God bless you in all your undertakings. I remain to be yours ever,
>
> Joshua Gewen Beso
>
> P.S. Please, the Matron said she came to Saboba and met your absence.

Joel Ubor Wumbei, who was admitted at the same time, wrote:

> In fact I have never seen women like the two of you, so pacific (calm) and kind, and now there are three. Barbara Liddle is also there. (Flattery, but nice!) Thank you for getting Gewen and me into this training program. I received your letters and it made me happy as the word happy itself! Tadimie wrote that he is in training in Tamale Hospital. He says they are learning to make beds. We are masters of beds, taking T.P.R. and blood pressure! In fact, we have learned things I was not sure we would ever learn! When we worked in Saboba Clinic, we thought we were working hard. Here we go from 7 P.M. to 1 A.M. in the night with standing only, no sitting down! I was so sorry to learn that our Matron went from here to Saboba and did not meet you—not even one of you! You know she is a busy woman and has no time to waste! Oh, I tell you, she was also very sorry! She will write you. Have the Saboba people begun to pipe water from the Oti River? I Peter 5:7. Amen. OH, WHEN SHALL WE MEET AND LAUGH AGAIN! Until we meet Christmas day in Saboba!
>
> Yours only,
Joel Ubor Wumbei
>
> P.S. My best greeting to Emmanuel, Solomon, and all clinic workers and friends. When are you coming to Bawku?

I was *sure* Matron would write us! I considered my ear pulled! Joel had learned the fine art of ear pulling by watching U Na Febor Jayom, Chief of Yankazia, settle palavers (disputes). The flattery at the beginning of his letter was just to prepare us! However, I remembered how I felt when we arrived in Saboba and were told the matron had met our absence! I was very sorry too! She had been the epitome of kindness in admitting Joel and Gewen.

While we were passing through Accra on our return from Lome, I talked with Contractor Kofi about some other work to be done in Saboba. We talked about rebuilding clinic waiting sheds, a snakebite room where the mud and rock ones had fallen down, a library for youth activities and pastors' meetings, a watchman's quarters where ours had fallen down, a garage for two vehicles, parsonages at the Turner and Yankazia Churches, and fences around our yard and clinic buildings. Several of the churches needed benches before dedications. All those plans demanded another trek to Tamale for supplies and to bring Contractor Kofi to Saboba. I could not believe we were building again, and Christmas was creeping up fast! One Tuesday, on my way to Tamale, I stopped at Yendi Hospital where I dropped off our yard-man, Abraham, with his son, Herunah, to see Dr. Korsah. Mattah, Herunah's mom, had brought him to our clinic with joint pains many times and he was so thin; we suspected sickle-cell anemia.

I drove right on through Tamale to Kumbungu to ask permission of Franklin McCorkle to do the larger projects; he was back in Ghana and on the Missions Committee again. In addition, I had brought US surplus food for NGBS students and a Women's Retreat coming soon in Kumbungu. The next morning at a lumberyard in Tamale, Kofi and I ordered the needed lumber, all in metric measurements. I hunted for a lorry and driver for hire to haul the building supplies to Saboba. This included the lumber, cement, nails, paint, hinges, glass louvers and frames, white wash, and selignum (creosote) to deter termites. I went looking for aluminum roofing sheets. I was told there was none in Ghana. A Mr. Kasadzan said he would hunt for some in Accra, but that did not get them on the truck already hired! Then I went hunting at outdoor markets for bananas, a pineapple, paw paws, and Cokes. I filled two 45-gallon petrol (gasoline) drums in the back of the pickup. By then, the hired truck was far ahead with no waybill for checkpoints! I rushed to overtake the rambling vehicle and we got to Saboba about 6 P.M. on the third day of traveling. I had actually not eaten since the day before! There was mail but I was almost too tired to read it. I did notice a letter from Everett and Dorothy Phillips. She had written it from the airport in Abidjan, Ivory Coast. They were expressing their thanks for our efforts to be in Lome, Toga in their honor. They said we were spoiling them, and that was because they spoiled us!

We vowed to forget the building process until after the holidays. Contractor Kofi would not let us do that! If we ran out of supplies for him, he would return to the south and we'd never get him up here again! However, we did go to Sunson and buy a Christmas turkey. As late as December 23, we saw forty women at the maternity clinic in the morning. For some reason that I do not recall, Ann and I had harsh words; we were all over-extended. She left the clinic in tears. I had vowed I would not wait if I felt I had hurt her. I left the clinic and followed her to her room; we cried together. I can't remember that it ever happened again. After the clinic and our noon meal, we hauled sand and water in order not to hold up Kofi's work. Many young people on Christmas leave from their boarding schools were helping us get water from the pond for building. We drove; they filled and emptied the barrels. That was their contribution toward progress.

తు తు తు

One evening we had the annual Christmas feast of goat gravy and rice that Amos Biyimba cooked. It always took place on our *palaver porch* for our workers, Kofi's workers, the pastors, and their families, but students returning from boarding schools and others were included. Peter Kpolou came from the school in Kumasi. He said John Kitinyaab had also come but had gone to greet his father and family and would be coming to Saboba later.

We started the serious celebration on Wednesday, Christmas Eve, at Kokonzoli. Ann and Barbara took some schoolboys and girls with them in Ann's pickup ahead of me. They were to make tea. I came afterwards in the VW with more young students and we brought bread. We had oranges for the children; some had never seen one. I gave the Word at their lovely new church by telling *why Jesus came*, not just the story of His birth. Then we roamed! Yes, they did not call it caroling. We *went roaming* for about three miles. Ann and Barbara could keep up with Nado, Wumbidi, and all the young members from Kokonzoli. I was slower so Pastor Dahamani, Joel Ubor, Bikanyi, Peter Kwaku, Daniel Damba, and John Kitinyaab roamed a little slower with me. They had storm lanterns and we had flashlights. Nothing gave enough light to see a snake; we had to forget about snakes. (Ann edited this and said, "Who forgot?") They led us to the houses of the most important people in their villages and the young people themselves told them what the roaming was about. We returned to the Kokonzoli church, ate bread, drank hot tea while they sang, and circled a campfire. This scenario was repeated anywhere we went Wednesday through Sunday that week. On Christmas Day, Thursday, Barbara went back to Kokonzoli in the VW with Phillip Wumbei, Gewen Beso, and Simon Asore. Simon was a visiting Bible School student who was soon to be the pastor of Turner Chapel. (How could we possibly know that Pastor Simon Asore would be the next Ghana Assemblies of God General Superintendent following the retirement of Rev. E.J. Namyela?) Ann and I drove west where we were stuck on the talcum powder way for just a moment. Ann exited at Gbenja with Emmanuel Gondow and Dorcas Njonabi. I went on to Yankazia with Solomon King Binambo and Joel Ubor. David Mankrom Nabegmado was already there. Teacher Samson Mankrom had come from Tamale to be with his extended family for

Christmas. He interpreted for me as I gave the Word. Before we left, U Na Febor Jayom (Chief) dashed us some yams and a guinea foul as his Christmas gifts.

When we all returned on Christmas Day, we ate a late lunch. Amos Biyimba, our cook, was off for Christmas Day. All afternoon our workers and families came to greet us; we received and gave small gifts. We had already given the house and clinic workers a bonus of NC10 for Christmas. After the people almost stopped coming, we opened our personal Christmas gifts. On Christmas evening, there was a presentation at the Toma Church. Ann and Barbara went. I was at the clinic with a woman who came in premature labor. I started sedation and had a woman to sit with her when a seven-year-old boy came with a bad snakebite on the hand. He was vomiting blood already. I gave him two ampoules of anti-venom serum in the vein before the clotting power of the blood reversed. I really did not have time to decide whether he was allergic or sensitive to the treatment. I decided one or two more holes to bleed from would probably not be the killing factor if he died, so I gave him Benadryl and Vitamin K in the muscle. He was scared, so I gave him codeine to help him tolerate all the needles coming at him. Finally, he slept and the next day he was much improved.

The day after Christmas six visitors came to our house. They were Anne Symonds and Becky Davison from Yendi, Joy King and Sharon Wallace from Nakpanduri Clinic, and Charley Pearson and Franklin McCorkle from NGBI in Kumbungu. Amos Biyimba came back to work and cooked the huge turkey with all the trimmings we had saved or could find in a tin can, cardboard box, or the local market. As we were finishing our meal from a freezer of ice cream for desert, someone started and we all joined in declaring, "Behold how we suffer!" On Saturday, Franklin McCorkle helped to square off for the foundation of the library and youth center. Joy and Sharon were the only ones who stayed overnight

Saturday. Joy King gave the Word on Sunday morning in the Toma Church. They ate lunch with us before they traveled back to Nakpanduri. They had a clinic to run the same as we.

On Monday after Christmas, Ann had a full general clinic while I went to Yendi to order five hundred bags of cement, sixty rebar rods, one hundred pounds of roofing nails, and three thousand plastic washers; that is what Kofi ordered. On Tuesday, we visited layman Kpalija's village with Pastor Namyela and prayed with them, as his wife had died. On Wednesday, we evaluated forty prenatal clients. We sent the child home that had come to the clinic on Christmas Eve with snakebite. Everyone at the clinic cheered when he left. We had worked hard to reverse the bleeding in that one!

Barbara drove to Tamale to get a tooth pulled. She took Makpa, Amos Biyimba's wife, as she needed dental work. Of course, the twins were small and had to be with their mother, so Hannah went to care for the second twin. She was still doing it without complaint. Thomas, Amos Biyimba's son just older than the twins, was brought to us that evening extremely ill. We treated him for both malaria and chest congestion. I believe we saved his life while his mother was in Tamale. Those were the rewarding times. When Barbara returned, she found a poem and some money under her pillow. The poem read:

We've sometimes heard that in one's youth,
One often times would loose a tooth.
And that at night the good, good, fairy,
Some small, small coins to them would carry.
Perhaps you thought this all a spoof,
Now for sure you know the truth!

Wednesday afternoon young people came to help load and unload as we hauled bricks and bags of cement to repair the Toma Church belfry and Sunday school rooms. They were Andrew Beso, James (Biyimba's nephew), John Uwum-barti, Gilbert Bukari (Pastor's nephew), Gideon and Susanna (Pastor's children), and Dorcas. I took the opportunity to get a picture of Dorcas, a teenager, holding a dishpan. I had a picture of her being bathed in that pan by her mother, when she was a few months old. That showed how long I had been in Africa.

༝ ༝ ༝

At 2 A.M. on the last day of 1970, Dundow awoke us, as the woman who came on Christmas Eve was in true labor. She delivered two hours later. The baby weighed three pounds and ten ounces; the wee lad survived! We went to a watch-night service at the Toma Church and prayed until 1971. The past year had been much more satisfying than 1969. We were tired, but we felt we had contributed positively to the greater Saboba Area. Students had to scramble to get back to their boarding schools in time for classes. We took some as far as Yendi when we traveled for more building material. Then letters started coming from them. Peter Kwaku wrote:

> Thank you for taking me to Yendi. I went on the mail car to Chinderi. My parents extend their greetings. I explained *Christmas in Saboba* and they were happy. Ani Libin poan (Happy New Year)!

Gideon Tadimie wrote:

> Happy New Year of 1971. I arrived in Tamale with God's help. I told the nursing sister about the bandages made by American women. She said they needed some and you may bring them. Thank you for the devotion books. I like those books even more than food.

CHAPTER FIVE

Church Dedications
Visitors from West Texas

ON THE FIRST SATURDAY of 1971, Contractor Kofi and
I drove by way of Yankazia to Yendi to coordinate
his building schedule with Yendi Anne and Becky.
We were back in Saboba by evening. On Sunday, Ann and
Barbara swam the "talcum powder way" to Kokonzoli for
Pastor Dahamani's last Sunday as pastor. I was tired, so I
walked one block to Turner Church for evening worship
with the few who already met in the impressive building,
although it was not yet dedicated. Simon Asore, on holiday
from NGBI, was already Acting Pastor. He would graduate
near the end of 1971 and be installed as the first pastor of
Turner Church. He came to Saboba on most holidays and
seemed to fit in well.

Oh, the woes of building! Kofi was keeping track of the
cement by saving the empty bags. We sold them to pay
workers. When a worker took four bags, empty or full, Kofi
sacked (fired) him on the spot! I suspect it was not worth
the loss of his income. We were amazed when a young man
told us to quit hauling water from the local dam that Dewey
Hale had helped make possible; we started hauling from the

117

Oti River. Days later, the young man came and said, "Mr. J.G. Amamo, the Deputy Minister of Health from Accra was coming to break ground for a *Government Health Center in Saboba."* He said that thirteen dignitaries from Accra, Tamale, Yendi, and Cheraponi would be coming to our house, the largest house near the groundbreaking site. Those arriving were the Deputy Minister of Health from Accra, Dr. Okonmah, Regional Medical Officer from Tamale, and a new District Medical Officer for Yendi Hospital; we were losing our great Dr. Korsah. The District Commissioner and Assistant District Commissioner came, as well as Assistant Superintendent of Police (ASP) from both Yendi and Saboba. The Town Council Chairman, who said he wanted our land, was there. Chief Quadin came with some of his councilmen and chiefs from surrounding villages. Men from the Ghana Information Service, who wrote the previous fine article about Saboba Clinic, were recording all. We served Cokes, ice water, and cookies.

We were called to the clinic at high noon, with the visitors still in our house; we left Barbara and Biyimba in charge. A small, teenage girl being treated for tuberculosis and hepatitis went into labor and delivered. When we determined the wee boy, a bit over three pounds, was very much alive, we joined the groundbreaking. Pictures were taken as shovels broke ground. Someone remarked, "These nurses have put Saboba on the map."

After the ceremonies, the Chairman of the Saboba Town Council took government officials on a boating trip. Some sort of accident happened. We were told that word was circulating, "After the hemorrhage at the Saboba Police Station and now the boating incident, you best keep your hands off those nurses." I said, "Never under estimate the power of prayer by Konkombas when they pray for God's help in their heavenly language!" Similar to the amazing Navajo Code Talkers in WWII, even the devil cannot de-code the heavenly language when God speaks.

~ ~ ~

On January 8, I was back in Tamale buying what was actually the last big load for building. We were putting the finishing touches to fourteen projects, including four churches. I bought the supplies from GNTC (Ghana National Trading Company). There were bags of cement, several bundles of aluminum roofing sheets, rolls of wire fence, a roll of barbed wire, and many iron rods. While I was thinking about how to transport the supplies, I drove out to Kumbungu to welcome Aniece back from helping her ailing, aged parents in Texas.

Back in Tamale I failed to find a lorry for hire at two lorry parks; we could not agree on a price. For a truck named, "Brain Behind," my load was not big enough. For one called "Everything by God," the journey to Saboba was not enough miles, yet it would tear his truck up on the bad roads and I could not pay over NC50 for his trip. I parked and prayed. In New Mexico, it was Mom and Dad's fiftieth wedding anniversary; I was feeling nostalgic. I had already sent money to my sister for flowers. Finally, I found a driver and lorry. I paid him NC45 and we were both happy. When he arrived in Saboba, the Manager of the GNTC Store was riding with him. The truck had over NC800 worth of merchandise and drivers had been known to take a load over the border and sell it for stable French Francs. I was learning!

The Mission Committee Chairman wrote us that Turner Church was to be dedicated January 14. That made two big celebrations within two weeks! On January 10, Pastor Namyela came to our house; we prepared a program. At 3 A.M., I did bookkeeping for church and clinic building projects and activities. Ann was sometimes getting little help from me at the clinic. It got too much for her, as she was worried about her mom. We decided that Ann must take a break, go to Tamale, and phone her parents in Texas. There was no turning back once you got into a building project. Like the loving husband says to his wife near to give birth, "Honey, are you sure you want to go through with this?"

While Ann and Barbara were gone, my day started at 6 A.M. I hauled two loads of water before eating breakfast. On one trip a fan belt broke. I found someone to help put on a new one and we hardly skipped a beat! We had prayer and reading of the Word on the palaver porch and everyone went to work. Dondow was painting around the *stained glass windows* at Turner. Amos Biyimba and Abraham Kusasi were waxing and polishing benches even as Kofi and his workers made them. David Brown and Solomon Wassah carried benches borrowed from the local middle school for the Turner celebration. We planned meals for those who came from afar; there were no fast food places! I went to the clinic where fifty-five people waited. The small mother and wee baby were among them. He still weighed less than four pounds, but both were fine.

I treated thirty-six patients before Kofi called for more water. The people from the village of Sobiba, a few miles from Saboba, sent word that there were many women and children in their village who were having diarrhea; they were afraid it might be cholera. We had given all the cholera immunizations the government had supplied. We gave them medicine to give to their women and children, and told them to come back if it did not solve the problem. After seeing the last patient, Dondow went back to painting Turner window frames. Contractor Kofi must return to the coast on a certain date.

Late in the afternoon, Pastor Namyela and I delivered invitations to chiefs' compounds, the market area, police station, schools, and the Catholic Mission. We specifically took one to the man who had asked us to give up our land. He told us what we had already heard, about his near drowning with two Government Ministers on groundbreaking day. We went to Gylima and Bikanti Akonsi, my prized former PhD clinic helper; he confessed his needs and asked for prayer.

Then we took invitations to the postmaster, agricultural officer, education officer, head butcher, and to Issaka Timbila, the beloved mail-and-market lorry driver; he was Muslim. I went to bed with muscle spasms in my back and down my legs from walking. I "took two aspirin and called me in the morning!" Who else could I call?

On Tuesday, we worked all day with Kofi to get Turner Chapel ready. Late in the evening, I was called to the clinic for a woman in premature labor. As David Brown and I walked toward my house and Abraham was turning off the diesel engine, a car drove up; it was Jim and Delta Kessler from Accra. Jim was Chairman of the Mission Committee. Abraham sparked the generator again and we had lights. I showed the Kesslers to Ann's sleeping quarters and gave them copies of the invitation and program for approval. Amos was still working in the kitchen; I helped him grind beef for meat loaves he would bake the next day. Wednesday morning there were forty-seven women for maternity checkups. When clinic was over, Chief Quadin called me to his compound; he was concerned about possible cholera at Sobiba. Ann and Barbara returned from Tamale that day and we went to the suspect village to collect specimen to send to Yendi for cholera testing. The results were negative, but we got more cholera vaccine because of the scare.

Thursday, January 14, was D-Day! At 2 P.M., Turner Chapel was dedicated. The building was impressive indeed! It was more like a memorial service for Virginia Turner. I did wish the family knew how very hard our house and clinic workers, as well as Ann, Barbara, and I had worked. I hope they were told how hard Contractor Samuel Kofi and his workers, Pastor Namyela and his family, and the whole Toma Church membership worked. The last minute, I typed changes on the program and duplicated them. Most of the Northern Ghana missionaries came: Franklin and Aniece McCorkle and Charley Pearson from Kumbungu; Ed and Faith (Weidman) Ferguson with Paula, Rickie, and Scottie from Tamale; Anne Symonds and Becky Davison from Yendi; Joy King and Sharon Wallace from Nakpanduri, and the three of us. I believe Arthur and Doris Hokett, from Wale-wale, were not there because Jeff, their newborn, was too young. However, Pastor Tiga Ouedraogo, a true Mosi-man from Upper Volta, came. He was pastor at Pong Tamale near Walewale. Pastor Namyela and the local Christians fed the visiting Ghanaians. We fed thirteen adults and three children with Biyimba's delicious meat loaves.

At the ceremony, Saboba-Yendi Sectional Presbyter T.Y. Dokurugu opened with prayer in Dagbani. Rev. E.J. Namyela and David Brown interpreted for the day's activities. Ann and I welcomed and acknowledged the visitors. We, along with Jim Kessler, especially honored Contractor Samuel Kofi and his crew! Sharon Wallace gave a tribute to Virginia Turner. Revs. Kessler and McCorkle conducted both the inside and outside acts of dedication. Jim Kessler preached the dedication sermon titled, "She (referring to Virginia Turner) hath done what she could." It was good! In Lekpakpaln it was, "U pung umung paa!" Literal: She tried herself! The Toma Church youth choir, lead by Ann, sang, "We Bow to Thee," taught to them by David and Gretchen Kast, from Lesotho, on a visit. Barbara Liddle sang, "Then Jesus Came." The congregation sang, "N Dinda, Ma Ga Sun Ke Pag Si." The song said, "MY Lord, I will not forget to pray (or praise) Thee." I believe Samson Mankrom, of Yankazia, wrote that. For the dedication of the house by the congregation, E.J. Namyela read and David Brown led the congregation in the Lekpakpaln Response: *"Ta Uwumbor ti tisi Kidike," (Our God we give you this house).

- Minister: With Thanksgiving for those who labored, prayed, and contributed of their finances to build this church,

- Response: *Ti Uwumbor ti tisi Kidike.

- Minister: That people may hear the Word of God and be brought to Jesus and their faith be made strong, (* Response)

- Minister: For the comfort of those who mourn, for strengthening of those who are weak, for the helping of any who are tempted and tried, (* Response)

- Minister: That this house shall be used to give praise to God the Father, God the Son, and God the Holy Ghost, (* Response)

Chief Quadin gave a response for the town of Saboba in accepting the beautiful building as a positive addition to their town. The outside ribbon cutting ceremony followed. Rev. Tiga Ouedraogo pronounced the benediction. An offering received by Franklin McCorkle was to provide more benches.

The next morning was Friday. Pastors Namyela and Simon Asore came with a list of possible church officers and Sunday school teachers. Some who qualified lived near Toma Church, some near Turner Chapel. We planned a schedule for each church, and who would be in charge. Simon Asore would still be in NGBI for a while, so Pastor Namyela, his time already overloaded, would need to preach at both places for a time. The first evening I saw the Turner Church lit up for worship, it looked so beautiful! They had their mandate.

January 17 was the first official Sunday morning service for Turner Chapel. Namyela preached in English and Dondow interpreted into the local Lekpakpaln. Pastor said that while we were in a magnificent building, we must know reality. The church was for ministering to people, to present a WAY for them to stand before God when the time came. He quoted Jesus who said, "I am the Way." Finally, he said that God's Son was man's only salvation; that's why it is called *being saved*. He emphasized again, "We are here for the people; never forgetting our purpose for being *the church*, which a building is not!"

In that one service, we sang in English (for coastal tribesmen present), Twi (for Ashanti forest tribesmen), Lekpakpaln (for Konkomba tribesmen), Dagbani (for Dagomba and trader tribesmen), and Mampruli (Namyela's Mamprusi tribesmen). Simon Azore, a Busanga by tribe, had come with the McCorkles to the dedication and stayed over until he his school started. He would not be installed until he graduated, but he prayed the benediction in his Busanga language. Six languages in one service! It was instantly evident that God had met a need without our realizing it existed! Many tribes had moved into Saboba for as many reasons. It was a border town. Amos Biyimba, I believe, was to be Superintendent of the Turner Sunday school; he could speak English and Lekpakpaln and understand even more. Teachers, for the moment, were Men's class, Dondow; Women's class, Spencer and David Brown Magbaan, interpreter; Youth class, Fisher and Gladys Mankrom (Simon Asore for that day as Gladys was absent); Children's class, Helen Beso Magbaan and Job. Job was so excited; he was from nearby Kpatapaab, the chief's compound. It was a church for all!

On the other hand, the Toma Church was definitely in a Konkomba village community. It was in the midst of the first families to accept Jesus as the Christ and God's Sacrifice for sins. I could not help but remember when we had to abandon the first mud church in Saboba because they had outgrown it, the snakes were taking over, and it was about to fall down. It was located halfway between these two present churches. What a great thing the Toma people had started! May their church stand many years. Years later, Rev. David M. Nabegmado told me, "The Toma Church is still strong. The Turner Church is now the youth hall and a larger tabernacle stands beside it to seat the people for worship."

♋ ♋ ♋

In January 1971, among all the celebration, we received letters from the Saboba young people who were off in schools. No grass grew under the feet of Joshua Gewen Beso; he was always on the lookout for advancement. He wrote asking us to look for an advanced nursing program. We were thinking another way; he may be needed at Saboba clinic when we left on furlough. His letter continued, "We told Matron what you said (about her meeting your absence). She was pleased to hear it. Greet the workers for me. God bless and bye, bye; I remain to be yours in Christ, JGB." He went another route and got his advanced nursing and I was proud of him! In a letter from Jacob Kotin at St. John Bosco's College in Navrongo, he complained of hot days and cold nights in the harmattan, but guessed correctly that Saboba was "in the same soup."

One day, The Pastor Lekpamba at Gbenja surprised us with a different kind of letter. Ann had especially visited him after he wrote how his *heart fell down* when he lost a child in September 1970. His people paid their tithes in kind, like grain, yams, or a fowl, but he still had little money. Yet, he said, "I am glad to be writing, as yesterday I received the baptism of the Holy Spirit. Yours faithfully, Lekpamba." He was a changed man!

Ngmakaan N. David wrote us from his position in "Forestry" on the way to Bole Animal Park. He sent special greetings to Pastor Lekpamba, so he should be happy that he had done something right! Then, in a letter from Joel Ubor he was pulling our ear nicely again. We had not kept them informed about church dedications and they heard it from another source! Also, we had not written the matron of our intention to visit Bawku and when. He said, "Read I Peter 5:7."

Early on Monday, January 18, a lorry came with our one hundred gallons of kerosene, sixty gallons of diesel, and *a lorry fee on top!* After prayer with workers on the palaver porch, Ann went to haul water so I could have the pickup later. She returned and went to the clinic. I left with ten women for

Women's Retreat at NGBI in Kumbungu. They were Kwosia from Toma, Karen Namyela with Joy, Helen Brown with Joseph, Bagi Likpamba with Naomi, Makpa Biyimba with Peter and Phillip (and Hannah!), Nanabikina Dondow with Mary Charlese, Mattah with Isaac, Nyimakai's wife and two women from Kokonzoli. Back home from that trip, I became terribly ill with malaria even while taking Chloroquin. Three partridges came for water safely; I was too ill to use my gun. As often happened, one week after my illness, Ann became ill with malaria. We were to leave at 6 a.m. the next morning to go to Kumbungu for Northern District Council. Over a heavy game of Yahtzee that evening, we decided that Barbara should go first to take the pastors early for committee meetings. Ann would feel better to travel by Saturday. Barbara would not return to Saboba after District Council, but would go to help at a school in Liberia. We would miss her!

Ann improved enough to help a bit with clinic by Friday. We had two bad burn cases, a man and a woman; two teenagers died in that fire. There was a teenager with snakebite, a woman in premature labor, and two new mothers and babies staying at the clinic for observation. After general clinic, I hauled water, paid our workers a day early, and wrote letters to mail in Tamale. I wrote my brother, Lee, for his birthday and drew a valentine for my nephew, Kevin. A stick figure inside a red heart flailed its arms and exclaiming, "What do you mean, February 14; you're my valentine 365 days a year!" An African proverb says, "Necessity compels a butcher to kill a cat!" We could not buy cards!

We drove to Tamale late Saturday. Amos went with us as required for conventions. In Tamale, Ann and I rested on Sunday, as we were still not too well. In fact, Ann was vomiting again. After the District Council Ann, Biyimba, the pastors, and I went back to Saboba in our two lorries. Barbara went to Liberia. She was with us seven months and had been a big help, especially in Religious Education Classes in Ghana Government Schools during our heavy building program. I believe Ann really enjoyed having someone younger in the house for a time. Actually, we missed Barbara terribly!

Kofi was saying he must go south. He had been in Saboba to build the new churches from April to June, less than three months. The second time he stayed less than two months, but some of his workers joined in our roaming (caroling) for Christmas.

On February 11, a pastors' meeting lasted all day. The next day Pastor Namyela, Pastor Dahamani, a local carpenter, and I drove to Yankazia to get that church ready to dedicate. We took paint and left Pastor Dahamani to help Pastor Abarika. We left the carpenter to repair benches. Namyela and I drove to Kokonzoli to see if they were ready for their church dedication.

On February 13, I worked on a picture letter to be sent to relatives and friends. I wrote two lines of verses for each picture. They read:

You've sent us here to Speed-the-Light.
And so we try with all our might.
We load the bug, Ah, what a sight!
But must respect the water's height.

Of clinic tasks we talk and talk.
When called at night we feel to balk.
But efforts pay; our fears we mock,
When darling Helen now can walk!

Each one must help if we're to build.
For this huge task, we were not drilled.
Four churches finished; we are thrilled!
Before completion, some were filled.

Sometimes the babies come by two.
How dear they are when they are new.
Phillip and Peter (& Hannah) greeting you,
"Without your help what would we do?"

My dad wrote me on Valentine's Day; I was delighted. It may have been the nicest and longest letter I ever received from him. He was telling me about their fiftieth anniversary celebration and thanking me for the flowers. He told me about good times and hardships at the ranch. He reported on their animals from my mom's piglet inside the house to his dogs outside.

∽ ∽ ∽

On February 16, we had a delivery at 7:15 A.M. before young Matthew came to tell us a doctor for cholera education was in town. We went for a meeting with them and they appointed us on a committee for the area, so now we would not bear the cholera problem alone! When the meeting adjourned, we drove to Yendi for the wedding of Yajoningan, the girl who was kidnapped earlier, and Samson. He was a self-taught, no formal schooling, Sunday School Superintendent at a village church south of Yendi. Samson and Yajoningan wrote me in America when their first son was born. After the wedding in Yendi, we drove on to Tamale in both vehicles for two reasons. We took Kofi and his crew to Tamale, where they could get a lorry going south. Franklin McCorkle said the NGBI bus had broken down and that there were those who wanted to go for the dedications of the Kokonzoli and Yankazia churches the next two days. It was already 5 p.m. Ann drove the pickup while I followed in the Wee Dubya; I could hardly keep up! When I asked Ann why she drove so fast, she said, "I guess I had just finally learned to do so!" Actually, we just wanted to get home! We were back in Saboba with our passengers by midnight.

We evaluated over sixty women in the maternity clinic on Wednesday before going to the Kokonzoli dedication at 2 P.M. The ceremony progressed as planned. By request from the Kokonzoli laymen, they used the same format as at the Turner Church. Rev. Namyela and Rev. McCorkle conducted the ceremony and gave the addresses. They both spoke in English and Dagbani. One man interpreted for those who spoke only Lekpakpaln. The local people fed the visitors rice with rabbit gravy.

For that evening, back in Saboba, Franklin and Aniece showed a movie, *The End of Time*. They projected it on the white outside wall of the new library-youth-center between our house and Turner Church; many people came to see it. We served cake and tea to the visiting pastors. They were Revs. Daniel Wumbie, Awindow, Namyela, Dokurugu, and Yakubu, who became the new pastor of Kokonzoli and Teacher Mullings from NGBI. We were grateful for a bed that night and slept well.

Reality struck early next morning. We had one more church dedication that very day, the 18th. We heard Pastor Namyela bartering with Issaka for his lorry to take Saboba Church members to the Yankazia Church dedication. The fee was set and everyone went for a happy day. One end of the Yankazia Church building even had a colored glass cross in the wall, pieces left from the Turner Church. That was Contractor Kofi's idea totally. The same format was used for the third dedication, as many of the people had attended the Turner Chapel dedication and liked it. The District Superintendent E.J. Namyela, Franklin McCorkle, and Presbyter Dokurugu spoke and conducted the ceremonies. U Na Febor Jeyom (chief) was honored, for he had broken ground with Presbyter Dokurugu months ago. This was the third church built in Yankazia that took blood, sweat, and tears. This one was built with cement! Visitors overflowed it.

In spite of our fatigue, we had to pack a suitcase that night. When we finally retired, both of us were nauseated.

Besides taking the group back to Tamale the next day, we had to go straight from there to Accra for the Annual Mission Conference. Bronnie Stroud was elected to be Mission Committee Chairman for the next year. This term, he and Annabelle were teaching at Southern Ghana Bible Institute in Saltpond on the coast. Ann and I would be due for a furlough before next conference, so we presented our letter to the Mission Chairman for approval to return to Ghana later. We asked permission for Ann to receive her midwifery training and for me to work toward my Masters Degree in Nursing before returning to Ghana. This would probably take one year besides our regular furlough. They approved our return, but said the schooling would depend on how badly we were needed in Ghana. The signs we ordered in Accra and took north eventually were put on new church and clinic buildings.

☞ ☞ ☞

Around March 1, we were called to Tamale for a special meeting with Morris Williams, the new Secretary for all of Africa. Everett Phillips had retired. This made the third person serving in that capacity since I was approved for Africa in 1953. After that meeting, Ann and I finally went to Bawku to visit Joshua Gewen, Joel Ubor, and of course, the Matron who *met our absence* in Saboba. On our way back to Saboba, we stopped in Nakpanduri to visit Joy and Sharon. They took us to greet the Chief at Bunkpurugu. He was Nyankpen Libagitib, my former Nakpanduri Clinic helper. He was among the ones who were beaten in Najong #2 in 1959. We were told that, as Chief of Bunkpurugu, he was now automatically the highest chief of the Bimobas. That made him chief over those who once beat him. After that visit, Ann and I drove down the Gushiago moto'way, a short cut to Saboba.

There was a letter from Peter Kwaku. We had written how sorry we were that his father, Kpolou, had died. His greeting said, "Nidonaa," just "Good Morning." He said he felt better after reading the Ghana Evangel we sent. Gideon Tadimie wrote from Tamale. He said he was very sorry when he heard of the departure of Miss Liddle. He said, "I will try on my magic carpet and come to Saboba on Friday, 27th to get some food from my father which is too costly in Tamale, *so suspect me!*" He was such a delight! While Tadimie was training in Tamale, his father, Jagir, would often come from Kpatapaab, Chief Quadin's village, to our house. He was a member of the Chief's Council. He would ask us, "Have you been to Tamale?" He may know we went. He would ask, "Did you see Tadimie?" If we had been there, I would tell him what we knew about Tadimie. If it had kept long that we had not been to Tamale, Jagir would come and ask, "When are you going to Tamale?" He may know we were going soon. He would say, "Tell him there are many things to distract a young man. He must keep his mind on the things he went there to learn." I would promise to tell Tadimie. Tadimie replied in one of his letters, "I shall stick to the admonitions given to me by my father and you." Then we heard from Teacher J.Y. Joshua, Tadimie's friend, at Tatingyili, via Zabzugu. He said he planned, as instructed in a letter from us, to go to the house of the Lord and present his soul for strengthening. He said about forty people attended where he went. He added, "I was informed that at Kumbungu we have twenty-one students, out of which only three are not yet filled with the Holy Spirit." (Franklin McCorkle said the other three were filled later in the school chapel when MAPS Teacher Charley Pearson was healed of diagnosed, serious hepatitis.)

Gewen and Joel wasted no time in writing after our visit. Gewen wrote:

Your visit is like a dream. I can't believe you came to Bawku and paid us a visit.

Joel wrote:

I am very sorry to tell you this but I must. On the 22nd, I was sleeping outside, as it was so hot in Bawku. A thief came into my room and took my box. Thank God, the thief did not kill me! The box had my middle school certificate, books, watch, and uniform provided by our matron. As a friend walked from Missiga Village to the hospital the next day, he found books and papers on the road. He saw my name on a certificate and brought the things to me. The uniform, watch, and other items were gone. How can I work in the hospital without my watch to take pulse and respirations? My God knows today and forever. He is wonderful and big! Matron gave me a new uniform; friends gave me things. The thief did not know what damage he was doing. I pray to God to forgive him. Isaiah 59:1–3. I must tell you two miracles. While working in the hospital, a child was very, very sick. I did not know what to do, but I remembered God. I prayed for this child and on the same day, the condition of the child became better. He should have been dead, but within two days, the child who could not laugh was laughing. Then, it was one week before time for our government allowance and my money got finished. I went to the church and prayed. As I walked home, I met a friend. I asked him for just 2NP to buy sugar to make rice water, but he gave me 30NP instead. These are two of many things the Lord has done for me in Bawku. Greet Pastor Abarika in Yankazia. We will be coming home for our off-days June 26 to July 18. We hope to enjoy it with you, as you two will be going home to America before we have another leave at Christmas 1971. OH, WHEN SHALL WE

MEET AND LAUGH AGAIN? Joel. A note: Gewen and I passed the six-month probation period, so both will be allowed to stay in school.

That sounded like nursing!

❧ ❧ ❧

On Easter Sunday, we visited the local and outstation churches by splitting up and taking African helpers along. Simon Asore had come from NGBI to be with the people in Turner Church. The people in the Toma and Turner Churches joined for the sunrise service on the usual hill west of Saboba.

On Monday, April 12, I treated fifty people before lunch. Ann had gone to Tamale to have the pickup's gas tank welded. She took Jabob and his wife to NGBI for their first year. Simon Asore went to greet his family before returning to NGBI to complete his last year. Within a few days, he wrote from Kumbungu, "Thank you for getting us to school for this year." The people at Turner Chapel were helping him a bit, as he was coming back to be their pastor. He said:

> We are twenty-one students from nine tribes. There are seven Kusasis, five Bimobas, one Frafra, two Kasinas, three Mamprusis, one Ashanti, and one Busanga (that is I). One is a girl, a Krobo. We started classes on April 14. They are very surprised to see me playing the accordion. (Ann had taught him in her spare time inside the unfinished Turner Chapel.) Greet all your helpers at house, clinic, and the church.
>
> Simon M. Asore

On a Tuesday afternoon, I went to Yankazia with Pastor Namyela and a mason from Nigeria. We measured off for a parsonage for Pastor Abarika and family. I took mangos for the children. On the way back to Saboba, I hunted partridges in the twilight. That is why I did not see a pile of gravel emptied in the middle of the talcum powder way with no marker or warning. Pastor Namyela saw it and called a warning the same time I saw it, but it was too late. I swerved left and hit it with the right front tire. Gravel flew! It broke the right light glass. The fender was pushed back against the tire and locked it so it could not roll. We all hit our heads on the roof of the car. When we got the fender off the wheel and started on to Saboba, the horn honked each time I turned the steering wheel. It had gotten almost too dark to hunt, so I was like the proverbial horse heading for water. The next morning we had stiff necks and other sore spots. I had a big hematoma on my leg because of the steering wheel.

The next day was Wednesday; I evaluated fifty pregnant women. A thirteen-year-old boy arrived with snakebite. I gave him one ampoule of the anti-venom serum in the vein and thought I detected a change in clotting time. I went home to eat lunch and take a nap. When I awoke, Jim, Delta and Benny Kessler, from Accra, were waiting in my front room. They teased me about feeling that safe and had a message from Ann; the gas tank was still leaking. Delta went to the clinic twice with me that evening. I gave the snakebite lad the second ampoule of anti-venom serum; he was bleeding more than I had hoped. Then three men got patched up from a fight. I felt one man had bones broken, like a hand or clavicle that you can't do much about at the moment. I advised him to go to Yendi on a market lorry for x-rays; it was no emergency and my car was unfit!

The Kesslers had brought their son, Benny, to go hunting before he went away to school. Saboba was a good place to hunt. They got a waterbuck as big as an elk. They left most of the meat for the villagers where they killed it, but we ate meat for a long time. The Kesslers were sleeping out in Ann's room. At 3 a.m. in the morning, I heard hands clapping. A man reported he was driving a tractor when a passenger went to sleep and fell into the wheels. He asked me to go after the person. My car was damaged; I hated to go with the horn honking. Jim awoke and came to investigate. He said I did not need to go alone with a damaged car and a whiplashed neck among other aches and pains. He called his son, Benny, and the three of us went in Jim's car with the man. I sat in the backseat with the man. Jim was told when to stop. There was a house off in the bushes. The man was gone for a short while. He returned, saying that someone had come and taken the man to Yendi. However, when we got back to Saboba my car keys and change purse were gone. The man had taken them from the back seat even as we rode. I had extra keys but we half expected to wake up some morning and meet the absence of the little VW. I realized that I should have directed the man to Dundow. Locals knew not to come to my house, but to go to Dundow. Had I been alone, I would not have gone without Dundow; he may have suspected a hoax!

The next day was market day. Our workers asked people in the market about this stranger but they heard about neither him nor a tractor; no tractor accident was reported. We heard that two men from the coast had come to the home of a Baptist Nalerigu Hospital doctor. They told him a woman was in labor and could not get to the hospital. The doctor went with them. They drove him some ways, stripped him of his clothing, and made him give them the key to the hospital safe; they knew which doctor had keys! The doctor walked home; thank God, they did not kill him. The Saboba people said this could have been a similar situation, but the man hesitated when he saw Jim's hunting guns.

When Ann returned, I took the VW into Tamale for repairs from the accident. I told the man at UTC Garage that the horn was honking and they checked under the front of the car. In a few moments, they called me over and lifted one end of the steering rod straight up; it was broken in two. The break was on a slant and the bevel allowed it to turn the wheels. I had a Ghanaian with me. We had just driven over one hundred miles on some of the roughest roads in

Ghana; we chalked up another miracle. Ann was in Saboba alone and I was anxious to know how soon I could get the car repaired; he said it would not take long. I wrote for the money and said it was my first accident of any kind. Robert McGlassen replied that he hoped I drove another thirty years without a similar problem.

❧ ❧ ❧

One Wednesday, there were seventy maternity patients to evaluate. The next day we gave one hundred seventy cholera injections at the village of Sambuli. With no active building program, the two of us finished heavy clinics in a reasonable length of time. We had recently received an invitation from Joy and Sharon to a garden party the last of April in Nakpanduri. I was sure the invitation had to do with Ann and my birthday. We were gone only one day. A birthday card arrived from my sister. She said both my nephews, David and Kevin, were on TV and had their pictures in the *San Diego Sentinel*. They each won, in their age category, National Educational Television "Young Filmmakers Contest" awards. David, sixteen, produced *Circles*. Kevin, seven, produced *Super Glob*.

Tadimie Jagir passed the six-month probation and came to Saboba on leave for a few days in May; he could also continue in nursing. When he returned to Tamale Central Hospital, he wrote:

> I have cleaned my room, washed my dirty things and am ready for work on the 14th. I enjoyed working with you at the clinic during my holidays. I know you were not happy when I left, but we can't help it. We give everything to God in prayer and look for another time.

By May 29, we were in Tamale visiting him! Actually, we were driving to Accra to meet Ann's parents, Oren and Melba Fisher, from Lubbock, Texas. Her father was with her for the American Fathers' Day! They brought Ann a dress and material for a dress for me. They brought a package for me from the Kiddys, pastors in Eunice, New Mexico; they had moved from Santa Fe.

The trip by car from the coast and through the Ashanti Forest was very impressive to the Fishers. They seemed to enjoy it with some exceptions. First, we left Accra in the afternoon, so it was dark when we arrived in Kumasi in the Ashanti Forest. We left Kumasi in the afternoon so they could see the forest, but it was dark before we got to Tamale. We did the same when we left Tamale and got to Saboba in the dark. We tried to use the daylight for them to see things. Ann's father finally said, "I know why this place is often referred to as deep, darkest Africa. You two either leave, arrive, or both in the dark!" Second, at one time, it was a law that when you passed another lorry in the night, both must dim to their park lights. It was automatic with me. It was courtesy so both drivers could see in the terrible dust; bright lights glared and blinded in dust. If you did not do this, it could provoke road rage. Each time I switched the lights to park, Ann's father almost climbed over from the back seat. Driving on the left side of the road did not help! Most new missionaries went through those same reactions. I had been touted for twenty-three years, by Africans, Americans and missionary men, as one of the best and safest drivers in Africa and America. I had never even had a fender-bender itinerating in the USA or traveling in Africa, until I hit the gravel. My ego was deeply wounded.

When we finally reached Saboba, Ann's parents said they were pleasantly surprised at our living quarters. They meant it to be a compliment and we received it as such. We did, however, feel a bit like the old farmer who invited his pastor out for a visit. Each time he showed his pastor some part of the vast ranch, he got the same response, "My, but God has blessed and helped you!" After this same response several times, the farmer stopped, looked at his pastor, and said, "Hey, you should have seen this place when God had it by Himself!" I know! I know! God once had a Garden of Eden by Himself, too! He did not put a mud house in the middle of it and expect it never to fall down in a rainy season either! I believe it had not rained yet; dew came up from the ground. Ann and I had worked so hard. No one could possibly know what Ann saw at 9 p.m. on January 23, 1969 in the light of a storm lantern, or what more she saw by the next dawn's early light! No one could know what the place looked like later when it was an anthill of workers. The Fishers saw a beautiful church and a library in one direction. They saw a yard that looked like a lawn from Turner church to the library, past our house and down to the clinic. There was neither time nor a way to tell them what we had been through. We can never forget!

The gas tank to Ann's pickup was still leaking; the metal was rusted and riddled with holes. On a trip to Tamale, Ann's Dad mixed tubes of epoxy glue and coated the leaking gas tank; it never leaked again. Oren and Melba were in Saboba about a week. They loved the Saboba market; we thoroughly enjoyed watching them. Ann took them to a game reserve for a week. I stayed with the clinic. Pastor Namyela planned a week of teaching doctrine and Christian living in the two local churches and needed help. Outstation pastors attended so they could teach the course to their people. I liked what I saw, who was working in our house, at the clinics and in the churches. Young people were standing in the wings, ready for the challenge to take over!

On the following Tuesday, I drove to Tamale to meet Ann so we could see the Fishers off to America on a plane. What a wonderful visit! I saw why Joshua Gewen once said our visit to Bawku was like a dream. That's how I felt when Oren and Melba left. I'm sure I could only imagine how Ann felt. She may have kept telling herself that she would see them again near Christmas.

1. Yankazia's first church, in the chief's front room. Teacher Samson Mankrom, first pastor. 2. Clinic and waiting room (and Sunday school rooms). 3. Mud and metal roofed church. 4. Saboba and Kokonzoli Christians helping make cement blocks for permanent church. 5-6. A strong church and parsonage, with pastor Abarika and David Mankrom (Nabegmado). 7. Solomon K. Binambo, Bible School teacher and his father. 8. Dedication day 1971.

1. Second church (garage). 2. Toma's chief Odin, first Christian Akonsi, and his son Gylima (PhD). 3-4. Beloved Decon Beso, Akonsi's son and families. 5. Bileti's family (except kidnapped Yajoningan) and their vehicle. 6-7. Ann's girls camp and speaker, Barbara Liddle (Cavaness). 8. Wedding: Lasim, Gladys and O Na Febor Jeyom. 9. Last building dedicated. 10. Bye-bye to Ghana.

CHAPTER SIX

More Difficult Farewells

IN A BEAUTIFUL HANDWRITING, we received a letter from Kanton Training College in Tumu, Upper Region. It was from Gabriel Lasim. He said that he found favor in Gladys Mankrom and she in him. They intended wedding, "If God welcomes the situation, and if it meets your favor." Lasim said they would like to have the wedding within two months; that would be early September. He asked us to make a list of tasks and material necessary for the preparation. We promised to talk with Pastor Namyela and Gladys and keep him informed. It did not happen within two months!

∽ ∽ ∽

In July 1971, Gewen and Joel visited Saboba area on a short leave from nursing school in Bawku. They helped us at the clinic. After their return to school, Gewen wrote us about their trip:

Between Yendi and Tamale, a lorry *tyre* just gave an alarming explosion. The driver was able to control the lorry. Everybody was just frightened and semiconscious. The fifty miles from Bolgatanga to Bawku took three hours due to rain washing off the roads. We express

141

gratitude for your help and give the praise to God. We will not sit down dormant in praying for you. The scripture on the front of this page, is it not thrilling! "... we know that all things work together for good to them that love God." Romans 8:28. I have made Joel aware of my writing. He said I have gathered all his facts and am sending his words to you in absentia. Cheerio from Bawku.

Yours in Christ, JGB

John Kitinyaab Nampoah was finding it hard to get employment without more education. In July, we heard of a scholarship whereby we might get him back into the Institute of Planning & Technology with Peter Kpolou. Then, Emmanuel Gondow left a technical school because they were trying to switch him to carpentry. A company gave both John and Emmanuel a scholarship into IPT where Peter was. We stirred the water and grabbed every opportunity for tests or scholarships. I've been so proud to see what God did with David, Solomon, and Emmanuel; God knew what He planned. I took food to NGBI and sent money from New Mexico Churches for those Konkomba students, as well as for Jabab, Andrew, and others. The Principals acknowledged receiving the money. I fear Emmanuel chose the harder road and suffered; God has a reward for him!

～ ～ ～

Youth Camp, the highlight of each year and a spiritual must, took place in August of 1971. It was held in the Bawku area for both boys and girls. The teenagers cut grass as usual; they just about depleted our finances! That year, we hired Issaka's lorry with their money to transport them to Bawku. Since it was to be in the Bawku area, where Joshua and Joel were in nursing, we hoped they could attend. We forgot to inform Peter Kpolou and Teacher J.Y. Joshua south of Yendi. Keeping track of them was not easy! Actually, I was happy for the campers to cut grass. Once when I was using the rotary lawn mower to keep the grass down so we could see the snakes, a West African house snake bit me. They are only mildly poisonous. I was wearing thongs when I stepped backwards to get a good shove on the mower. It felt like a twig grabbed my foot. It never occurred to me that a snake bit me until I went into the house to wash off the dust. There were the familiar marks. On a trip to Tamale the next day, I discovered it was swollen; that was the end of it. A middle school boy was not so fortunate. A very poisonous snake bit him the same day in his village. We heard he was taken to a juju practitioner and finally to Yendi Hospital, where he died. We were very sad! However, two rewarding incidents also happened. First, at pre-clinic prayer, a PWD supervisor of roadwork in the area accepted Christ as his blood Sacrifice and pledged to make Jesus the Lord of his life. He became faithful in his attendance at Turner Church. His wife did not join him immediately; she followed later. Second, a woman was brought in with snakebite. Her baby was a month old. The mother bled from every small scratch and orifice and, in spite of anti-venom serum, she convulsed. We sedated her and asked permission to pray for her. Her husband agreed. From the time of prayer, her condition began to stabilize. Within a week, she put her baby on her back and walked home with family members.

We were eligible to go home soon, so we took John and Emmanuel to school near October 1 to make sure their scholarships were well activated before we went to America. Peter was there from leave and delighted to see his two friends. John Kitinyaab was now more serious about school. He wrote, "How was your journey back? I don't even know how to thank you people. I am expressing my thanks for how God instructed you to get me in here. I will try hard and you will hear of my success in America! I have gone into the second year instead of starting over. I think I should rather be challenged, than to be at the top of the first year class. Emmanuel will be in the first year class. I am now worrying about your leaving to America. I wish I could have you stay in Saboba, but I can't make that happen."

On Friday, October 22, 1971, the patient count of one hundred three may have been the highest for a general clinic day, unless we were giving hundreds of injections for cholera or DPT. At a late lunch, we ate all but our desert when visitors came. One was a new, young Dr. Quasia, the replacement for Dr. Korsah. Dr. Quasia had recently completed at Korle Bu Hospital School of Medicine in Accra. We took him to see Saboba Clinic facilities. An eclamptic mother from Zongo was an in-patient with a small premature baby under five pounds, her first. She had delivered earlier in the week, so was doing well. Her husband was staying with her. After the doctor left, we went to the house and ate our banana fritters for desert. We started to lie down for our afternoon rest when a schoolteacher brought a student with a dislocated knee. We told the teachers to get the injured student to Yendi for x-rays.

As we walked toward the house, we met Teacher Gabriel Lasim walking toward us. He had traveled from his teaching location to arrange for his pending wedding. It was decided that he and Gladys Mankrom of Yankazia would marry on November 20. He went on his way, and we went to our house. Daniel Damba Niwu and a young man called Anthony were helping us put books together for the Middle School Religious Instruction Classes. That was when Yakubu Timbila appeared to bid farewell. He had taken employment at Accra in research and was leaving Saboba. Suddenly our generator stopped an hour early. Abraham came to help us look for the problem. We found a short in the wiring to the new library. By cutting electricity to that building, the lights at the house and clinic came on. *More than nursing!* Timbila walked with Ann and me to the clinic where we made rounds and gave medications. Timbila left on a market lorry and we were left sad again.

All during October, we were packing in small ways as we were leaving on furlough the end of November. Activities of daily living had to continue. We were lowering stock at both house and clinic for inventory. I had malaria with the familiar temperature of 104F degrees, chest congestion, and a sore leg from a cholera shot. Yet in that month, we delivered eight babies. One was a girl, Deborah Ann, on the 10th for Mattah and Abraham (our yardman). They had Harunah, Isaac, and now a girl!

≈ ≈ ≈

One day I made a quick trip to Tamale about the wedding dress for Gladys. I delivered several items bought by people in Tamale because we were leaving. Back in Saboba, I went to bed early, as I was dead tired! I was drifting off to sleep when I heard Ann shut her door. She came as far as the door into my bedroom and I heard her gasp. I did not react at first. The second time she gasped, I was instantly wide-awake and asked, "Ann, do you see a snake?" Ann asked, "Charlese, are you teasing me?" Franklin McCorkle was a tease; Ann thought he had sent a rubber or plastic snake to tease her. I said, "No! Ann, if you see a snake it is real. Where is it?" She said, "Right in my pathway beside your bed." I said, "Watch it so it cannot disappear!" If you take your eyes off a snake, it is difficult to find again. I got out from under the mosquito net on the other side of my bed. I grabbed a broom and held the snake down for Ann to get a hoe and hammer his head! The snake was having trouble traveling on linoleum or he might have gotten away. It was the biggest carpet viper I had ever seen, and inside our house! The larger snakes, like the spitting cobra, might appear more frightening, but the carpet viper is more deadly. Their name describes them correctly; their backs are a beautiful pattern like a carpet. Ann got the water she came for and we both went to bed. It was October 30.

Sometime in the night, Dondow awoke us. Gylima Akonsi, my faithful clinic helper for so many years, died at 2 A.M. It broke my heart that they never called me before he died. I do not know who diagnosed his problem, but somewhere in my notes, it says *malignant melanoma*. Pastor Namyela arrived and asked us to transport Gylima's body in the pickup, passed the Toma Church to Nalongni, where a majority of his family lived. Maja, a senior of the family, said they could not bury Gylima until they could get a representative of their family from French Togo just across the Oti River. We sat with the family, waiting. Men were digging the grave. A runner returned and said the man they reached was old and sick; there was no one to come. Gylima was buried about noon. Bakanti, still a beautiful woman, was there with their daughters. I'm sure my heart could never hurt like theirs. I am pleased that I have good memories to record in my book. He helped his people in Saboba when there was no other who could have done what he did. He is in the hands of a just, loving, and merciful God; I hope to see Gylima again! Man sees the outside, only God can judge our hearts. Amos Biyimba wrote me years later when Gylima's wife, Bakanti, died; I was in the USA.

On Friday, November 12 in Tamale, I wrote my last letters home from Northern Ghana. We would be selling the VW, helping with a wedding, attending farewell services in all the churches, and packing. Clinic was held as usual, for we were not closing the clinic; Eloise Smith was coming. On a Saturday, I drove home with the wedding dress. That evening Ann and I made a bulletin board and painted a chair. Sunday, November 14 was our farewell service at Yankazia. We gave the bulletin board to the new church and the bamboo wicker chair to U Na Febor Jayom. We gradually had Catholic missionaries over for a farewell dinner, then the Wycliffe Marys and a tea for the Presbyterians.

The wedding of Lasim and Gladys was special. We designed the invitations and Gabriel and Gladys delivered them to their friends and family in Yankazia and many areas. They read:

Mr. Gabriel Nabuer Lasim and Miss Gladys Wumbei Mankrom respectfully request the pleasure of your company at their wedding on 20 November 1971 at 2 p.m. in First Assembly of God in Saboba. Reception and refreshments will follow in the parsonage.

We made an arch, wrapped it in white, and braided bougainvillea from our yard around it. Gladys wore the lovely bridal dress made by Mrs. Mutrage in Tamale. We even made a tiara with a small veil. We were not pushing this type of a wedding; they saw and heard about them around the world and wanted them! They did the same with style and sports! The other girls in the wedding wore their own African dresses. Lasim and Gladys were teachers and they wanted a special wedding. Ann, being young, made sure it was! The choir sang How Great Thou Art. Ann had taken a folding organ out with her and, at one time, had thought she would give it to NGBI, but had not done so. She played music as the participants walked down the aisle to the altar. The groom's attendant was Adam from the market area. The bridesmaid was Esther, one of Deacon Beso's daughters. O Na Febor Jayom, Chief of Yankazia, accompanied the bride down the aisle; she was his daughter. Samson Abarika, pastor at Yankazia, prayed God's blessings on the ceremony. Rev. Elijah Juam Namyela-Panka directed the couple in exchanging vows. They knelt while David Mankrom Nabegmado sang Submission, accompanied by Ann on the organ. Finally, Pastor Namyela-Panka prayed for them and introduced them as Mr. and Mrs. Gabriel Lasim. (The groom did not kiss the bride in front of the whole church! We did not see kissing in Africa, even between mothers and children. They showed love in more subtle ways.) Their letter followed:

We express our happiness and thanks to you both for untiring help. You have shown great concern for our well-being. Remember us in your prayers always as we do likewise. We are truly yours in Christ.

Mr. and Mrs. Lasim

We got teary-eyed.

ᏻ ᏻ ᏻ

Two historic events happened that November 20, 1971. We had a wedding, but also at 11 P.M., we delivered a baby boy, Wintuma, for Karen and Toma Pastor Namyela. Their son, Gideon, was so delighted; he now had a brother! He never ran to the bush as he had done each time another girl arrived! They were fortunate to have a boy, for out of the previous nineteen deliveries at the clinic, thirteen had been girls! Wintuma is the Mamprusi tribal word for *God's gift*. They called him Omega for a while, until they had two more boys, Enoch and Richmond, but no more girls!

The next day was Sunday, our farewell service at Turner Memorial Church. The compliments were so flattering that we thought surely they were speaking of someone else. However, when Dondow told how Helen wanted to walk upright and she was now doing so, I was wishing for a tape recorder; he was amazing. We were crying again!

We were getting farewell letters from many of those away at schools. Joshua Gewen wrote:

I should possibly say Christmas greetings because you are leaving before then. I am sad at your leaving, but you have kept long without seeing your parents. I wish I were there to see you leave. Remember us to your dear folks at home.

Gideon Tadimie wrote:

All bundles of papers I brought back with me for the patients got finished. I need more bundles because new patients are coming all the time. In early mornings when they awake, I see them reading the books. Even the nurses are asking for the books and the Evangel paper. I will not be happy when you go home. What can we do about all this? Imagine the kind of help you two have given the Konkomba young people this year. In fact, I am in shock! When you go, let it be as if we are still near each other.

Peter Kpolou wrote:

We shall be glad if God brings you to us again in Saboba after a few months in America. Pray for us to keep up with our studies. If I say all that is in me, this writing pad will get finished. This is the song we would like to sing for you, 'I am the Way the Truth and the Life;' that's what Jesus said. Without the Way, there is no going. Without the Truth, there is no knowing. Without the Life, there is no living. I am the Way, the Truth, and the Life; that's what Jesus said.' Merry Christmas!

John Kitinyaab wrote:

We are all very serious with our studies. I wish you were here to enjoy Christmas with us. This is to say my last words of farewell to both of you. In fact, as I write there are tears in my eyes as if I have lost you forever; it pains me very much. Even when I was in elementary school, we studied the Word of God together and went to give the Word to the villages like Nayil, Gbenja, and my own village. I feel I should hold you back in Saboba forever. I wish a group of CAs could sing and you tape it, so you can play it any time you feel for us. It is time for celebrating the anniversary of the death of an important chief from December 4 to 16. We have been warned not to be walking alone or leaving the college after 6:30 P.M., for they need the heads of human beings. Because of this, our Christmas vacation may start early. It is very serious and people must be aware; join us in prayer so that none of us is found a victim of this human sacrifice.

They did leave school early.

Bonnie Roll and Peggy Scott, workers with youth and Sunday Schools, came to Saboba on December 23, and stayed overnight. They had recovered from the accident quite well. It was common for missionaries to visit those who were scheduled to leave on furlough. It reduced stress and gave a bit of help with final tasks. Our visitors left on Wednesday and we drove over an almost impossible road to Kokonzoli for a farewell service. Again, we laughed and cried together. As I looked around and saw they were in this solid house, I was just grateful to God we were not leaving them as we found them. They gave us three guinea fowl. That night we were doubly thankful for a bed to fall into. As I often said, we hit the bed and bounced off. At thirty minutes past midnight, I delivered a baby boy for a young girl from Kumatiik; it was her first. I believe that to be the last baby I ever delivered at Saboba Clinic! We addressed Christmas cards until 3:30 A.M. and then slept until 6:30 A.M. After breakfast and devotions on the palaver porch, we paid and formally dismissed all workers except Abraham to watch the house and Dondow to treat emergencies at the clinic until Eloise arrived. I went for the last Religious Instruction class at the middle school and cried with the students.

The very last touch of the building program was when Abraham helped us put up the new signs bought months ago for the clinic, mission residence, and library. I wanted to be in Saboba about three more years and build nothing, just enjoy what we had built. We left it for Eloise to enjoy! After lunch and a short rest, Ann went to the last session of her Children's Hour at 2 P.M., said farewells, and cried with them. When she returned, we walked over to the market to sell some items. We were trying to get money to go to Jerusalem on our way home. One woman bought the dress I had on; I had to go home and change. She followed me and got her dress. That story may still be circulating in Saboba Market! We bartered for a lorry to take our drums to be stored in Tamale. A new mission printing press had been built in Accra; the old printing press building in Tamale was being used as a storeroom for those on furlough. Finally, we drove to Yankazia that evening to bid a last farewell to U Na Febor, Pastor Samson Abarika and family, David Mankrom, and Solomon Binambo.

On the last Saturday evening, I showed colored slides, using a whitewashed wall of the Library-Youth Center as a screen. People saw themselves as they helped build or repair fourteen structures in our three years. In spite of the abundance of bugs drawn to the electric lights, the people saw themselves carrying lumber, sacks of cement, huge bricks, and pans of mortar or water on their heads. Adults roared with laughter and children rolled on the ground in glee! Turner Church was between the youth center and the market. Our house was neatly fenced between the youth center and the fenced clinic buildings. The place looked nice, but we were tired!

On our last Sunday morning in Saboba, we went to Toma Church. Excuse me, I mean First Assembly! If we were wet with tears at the other church farewells, this one was more so. Some who spoke reminded us of Akonsi, the very first Christian in the tribe, as they were from his family. Some asked us to take greetings to the different nurses they had worked with. The nostalgia was almost unbearable. We loaded our vehicles later Sunday night, as we could not sleep. We planned to leave early Monday morning, but people just kept coming. Finally, we had coffee and cake with our helpers, followed by a time of devotion. Their "Bye-bye" was as overwhelming as their "Welcome, Madam!"

On Tuesday, November 30, 1971, I wrote in a letter on the plane: "We made it! We are on a plane from Tamale to Accra. What a sad, sad time and what a mad, mad rush." The touchdown in Kumasi was just for passengers to exit and board. We had not expected to get off at all until the stewardess said there were people to see us. Peter Kwaku, John Kitinyaab, and Emmanuel Gondow had footed it from the IPT and were waiting along with the local missionaries. Seeing these three young men gave us a boost of energy! We were ready for a great trip!

On December 1, Ann and I flew to Beirut, Lebanon with only a short stop in Cairo, Egypt. We had friends in Lebanon who did major road and bridge building in Ghana. They were preparing for Christmas by decorating the house at their ranch. There were grape arbors as far as you could see in every direction. I could not believe the size of grapes and other fruit on their table at all times! We stayed in a hotel in Beirut. Our hosts came to get us for touring Lebanon. The Bible speaks of the cedars of Lebanon; they took us to see them. Then our hosts drove us to Baalbeck, where massive temples were built of huge stones; no one seemed to know where the stones came from. They might have come from Solomon's temple in Jerusalem. We were told, "There were no stones like them in all of Lebanon." One day we took a bus tour to Damascus, Syria and back. Just at the border, there was a huge Coca-Cola sign that seemed totally out of place, except the words were in Arabic! Inside Damascus, a shopkeeper was drinking strong, hot tea with milk. I liked a small pan he was heating milk in more than commercial items on display; he sold it to me.

A plane could not fly directly from Lebanon to Israel; we went to the island of Cyprus. Before we boarded Middle East Airlines to Tel Aviv from Cyprus, we had the most thorough search of self and luggage imaginable! We landed in Tel Aviv, Israel, and were met by a taxi driver who drove us to Jerusalem. An owner of the Baptist Bookstore in Jerusalem had scheduled his father to drive us from one end of Israel to the other in his taxi. The son said, "My father is not one of us." We saw Israel from a Jewish point of view, very interesting! As we drove along the Jordan River from Jericho up to the Sea of Galilee, the driver stopped and took a soldier from one point to his next assignment. The driver explained that this was an obligation. The soldier said a bus, loaded with tourists, had exploded that day. We drove beside rolls of barbed wire several feet high; it stretched for miles. We spent the night in a hotel in Tiberius, as did our driver, and we ate Peter's fish, as all tourists must.

The next morning we drove through Nazareth to Haifa. When we passed a sign that pointed to Megiddo, we asked the driver to take us there. He said, "There is nothing there to see." We looked into the valley of Megiddo from a high hill on our way to Mt. Carmel. There, many years ago, the fire of God licked up water and Elijah's offering.

We visited Headquarters for the Bahai faith; they allowed Christians only as far as the foyer to read a plaque of explanation. The Haifa shipyards were massive and impressive. From there he drove down the Mediterranean coastline to Caesarea. After buying items in their shops, we turned southeast. I thought Hebron was interesting and awesome because of its age. We looked through holes in a floor at what we were told were the graves of Abraham and Leah. On our way back north to Bethlehem and Jerusalem, we saw where Rebecca was buried before they reached Hebron. The rolling hills around Bethlehem looked like a place where shepherds could *watch their flocks by night.*

The next morning, in our Jerusalem hotel, a group from England awakened us caroling in the halls. We knew we were very close to Christmas. I wrote cards to people in Africa and New Mexico, "I wish you a Merry Christmas from the Land of *The First Christmas.*"

We flew TWA from Jerusalem to Rome and observed Christmas in Italy. In three days we went shopping, visited

Vatican City, the catacombs where Christians were once forced to hide, and the prison where Paul died. A Pan American plane flew us to New York where we boarded a Boeing 747. It was intimidating; they expected that thing to fly! Ann and I were the only passengers in one of its huge compartments. I think we cried most of the way to Dallas. This was it! Nurse Ann Fisher and I, like Midwife Helen Kopp and I, had been through so much. It did not seem right to end so abruptly in a Dallas airport. Ann flew to Lubbock where her family met her. I flew to Albuquerque where my family met me at 11 p.m. They asked me what I wanted first. I said, "A hamburger and a Coke!" The next day Ann and I talked by phone. Ann asked, "What were you doing at midnight last night?" I replied, "Eating a hamburger and drinking a Coke." She said, "Me too!" Christmas decorations were up in America. We had seen the Twelve Days of Christmas, on *four continents!*

After being away three years, Christmas at home with family and long-time friends was very emotional. A Christmas box with three dresses from Mrs. Phi in Carlsbad's First Assembly was waiting at my parents' home. Boxed Holiday gifts or money in envelopes were waiting at the New Mexico District Council Office in Albuquerque. Among others, some were from the Redfearns in Alaska, Fred and Bonnie Chambers in Escondido, Lola Wilson in Anaheim, the James Brankels in Tucson, the W. Ken Stewarts in Dallas, Betty Olsen in Denver, Doris Stewart in Hobbs, the Jack Kites in Gran Quivera, and the Paul Savages in Albuquerque. I could hardly wait to itinerate and see everyone in many states! I felt they would be pleased to hear what Ann and I did with their money and our time in the past three years.

I learned that, without a spare bedroom in my parents' home, I could not stay there. The small house behind their home was rented, as was my house in Albuquerque. I wanted so much to be near my parents for the year of my furlough. I accidentally discovered a wee, two-bedroom house for sale on Morgan Street, about two blocks from my parents' home. I could get it from the woman for a very small down payment; her husband had died and she wanted to leave. A contract was drawn up that I felt I could live with. I called it my glorified apartment. I moved in and planned to do the *1/ night: 2/Sunday schedule* from there. Pastor Manning of Central Assembly in Albuquerque, who worked at Sears, helped me get a slightly damaged cook stove and furniture.

Ann Fisher's youngest sister, Linda Kay, was marrying Bob Tidwell on January 1, 1972. They had postponed their wedding so Ann could be there. I flew to Lubbock to celebrate with them. The third Fisher daughter, Janie, and her husband, Nolan Brown, had been married even before Ann and I went to Africa. We had a grand time remembering the visit Oren and Melba Fisher, Ann's parents, made to Saboba just months before!

❦ ❦ ❦

Within the first few months of 1972, letters from students scattered over Ghana in all kind of schools started coming; I prize them highly. Gideon Tadimie wrote:

> You may say this to your church (in America). I, Gideon Jagir Tadimie, want Madam Spencer and Madam Fisher to come back to Saboba in some time to come. Thank you for helping me into the Nursing Training School. It's not a help to me alone, but to my people also.

Spoken like a true son of a chief's council member! We knew we could never hire all those we helped; we were starting them on future careers. People helped me; I helped others! Tadimie added: "The tape recorder I bought from Miss Fisher has been stolen through a broken window. The police are investigating."

John Kitinyaab wrote:

Greetings from the campus of IPT. My father and all
my family extend warmest greetings to you. Not finding you in Saboba was a blow. 'Let not your heart be
troubled' comes to me. I have read MATT. 7:14-16 and I
pray God leads me through that narrow gate.

Peter Kpolou wrote:

I hope you found your family well. We three were very
sorry when you left us at the Kumasi airport. Thank you
for the postcards from the Holy City of Jerusalem.

Emmanuel Gondow wrote:

I am home for Christmas and the people were already
complaining that Miss Smith is not yet there and much
sickness is in Yankazia; no one is at Saboba to supply
David Mankrom with medications.

Hal and Naomi Lehmann had collected a small amount
of cedis for something they sold for Ann and me. They asked
what we wanted done with that small amount. Ann wrote
them that we decided it was to be given to Bonnie Roll and
Peggy Scott at Sunyani to help the IPT students. They followed through as instructed and the three students wrote to
express their appreciation. They also said that the two ladies
who brought the money were supplying them with devotional books as we had done before and they liked that.

My schedule for *once every night and twice on Sunday*
started seriously in February. It had to work around the
New Mexico District Council in early April and West Texas
District Council in Lubbock in late April. I wanted to be
there with Ann and her family. The New Mexico Ministers'
Seminar, which I could not miss, was May 8–10. My Dad's
birthday was June 4. I would be home for that and still get
to Kansas District Council June 11. My schedule was often
tight and difficult to follow. Fortunately, Rev. Lowenberg,
Kansas District Superintendent, was speaker at New Mexico District Council in April so we planned my schedule for

Kansas at that time. Fourteen Kansas Churches supported me regularly and many more sent support at times. I sent a list of those churches to the Kansas District Missions Secretary so he could schedule me around their calendar.

Rev. E.J. Namyela wrote from Saboba in March 1972:

> Miss Smith has come. The same people were starting to complain and trouble me about the closed clinic. It has ceased. Simon Asore graduated from NGBI and was installed as pastor of the new Turner Church in Saboba on February 12. Likewise, Rev. Yakubu has been installed as pastor in Kokonzoli. Pastor Lekpamba is going to pastor Caguyili, so Gbenja may be without a pastor. Jabab, the Bible school student, was trying hard with the village of Kijoni and the people will miss him as he returned to school at NGBI. Do you hear from Miss Fisher; has she started to midwifery school? The church people, clinic workers, Biyimba and family, and my family send their greetings. They say to hurry back. I have just returned from the fifty-year celebration of the Assemblies of God in Upper Volta (now Burkina Faso). There were about ten thousand people present. It was a wonder to hear Brother John Chastagner speak the Mori language of the Mosi people. Thank you for the bell for the church that you sent from Israel. Miss Smith brought it. Pastor Peter Yamusah, who is in school at WAAST for a higher degree, is coming to speak on Good Friday in Saboba.

> Yours in His Royal service, E.J. Namyela

In March 1972, Ann and I drove to the University of Mississippi to see about midwifery for her and a masters program for me. (UNM had no BS in nursing for me in 1952; they had no Masters Program for me in 1972.) The midwifery class in Mississippi was full! Ann did not apply for the following year as the mission said she could not stay home two years. The masters program had room for me, if I passed the SAT national exam. Hal Lehmann had been voted in as chairman of the Ghana Missions Committee; Ann reported all this to him. Hal replied:

> Joy King and Sharon Wallace are due to go on furlough in September 1973. I wish to emphasize the fact that at any time we have only one of the staff a registered midwife, we are operating on the edge of crisis and are dangerously near defaulting on our commitment to the Ghana Government. It would seem that if Ann takes the midwifery course and Charlese endeavors to raise funds for a new bungalow at Saboba, they would have their hands full.

(Hey, did I just notice permission to build a house for nurses?!)

> I also suggest that all nurses be required to raise fifty dollars per month in their budget for clinic operation. We agreed for that.

We nurses agreed with that too; most nurses spent food allowance for clinic needs. Hal was telling it like it was! He was trying to cope with the erratic midwifery problem of the clinics. The best laid plans of mice and of men--how little we all knew about the future!

My itinerary continued and in May, I found time to visit my only sister and her family, the Lynches, in San Diego and my Aunt Leonora Wister and family in Phoenix. I did not stay long as I had to be in Springfield, Missouri for the annual School of Missions the first week in June. Rev. Paul Lowenberg from Kansas was one of the speakers and his son, Doug, came with him. He was another of my long, tall nephews. The Lowenberg family and I always laughed about my not being a babysitter for Doug and Sandi in Wichita. I was old enough to be their mother, but they said I could be their companion.

From the School of Missions, I drove to Wichita for the Kansas District Council and stayed to itinerate. On June 17,

I took the Student Academic Test (SAT) at Wichita State. For some reason a lot of my mail was lost because of my traveling, and I received neither the results of the SAT nor a letter from the University of Mississippi. After District Council, I continued my Kansas itinerary. Not knowing whether I had passed or failed the test put me under stress. I phoned the University Medical Center in Jackson. The reply came in a burst, "Where are you? You have passed the SAT and have been accepted; you are to register today!" It was July 14. I phoned Robert McGlassen at the Division of Foreign Missions in Missouri. I canceled my Kansas itinerary, drove to Mississippi, and started school on July 17. A letter from Robert McGlassen followed to confirm our phone conversation. He said I must be ready to return to Ghana in September 1973 when Joy and Sharon left on furlough from Nakpanduri. That gave me only nine actual school months to complete the four-semester master's program. A Catholic Sister was assigned as my advisor; she understood my commitment. I registered for extra courses to fulfill the requirements of the school, keeping in mind the time element clearly stated by the mission. A student again! I declared that when St. Peter called the roll in heaven, I would probably reply, "Present Sir!"

The next letter from Hal Lehmann was almost smoking when it reached me. It was a copy of a letter he had written to Morris Williams at mission headquarters. He said:

> I heard today that Esther Miles, the coworker coming to be with Eloise, is neither permanent nor a nurse! Eloise has diabetes and is not well! I cannot believe, no matter how anxious Eloise was to return, that the Missions Department would allow this. Overwork causes sickness; sickness understandably affects disposition and social reaction.

Then young Konkomba men in the Saboba area wrote that Eloise Smith had another automobile accident. They

were in it! No one was killed. She lost control while driving the Bible School's VW Bus loaded with both boys and
girls for Youth Camp. The pastor's daughter from Kokonzoli
had a broken hand; that seemed to be the only broken bone.
Eloise had bad cuts on her back. They landed in water and
someone held her head out of the water so she could breathe
until help arrived. David Mankrom told me later that while
Eloise was in the hospital, he and several young people from
Saboba visited her. She said, "David, we must get some fertilizer to make you grow!" David said his peers jokingly
threatened him with fertilizer for years. They knew the true
story of why he was short. I was happy when Emmanuel
wrote from Northern Ghana Bible Institute at Kumbungu,
rather than IPT near Kumasi; it had to be his decision. He
said:

> Joel and Joshua have completed their nursing school
> in Bawku. Joel is at the Baptist Hospital at Nalerigu;
> Joshua Gewen is in Saboba A/G Clinic. I plan to pastor
> the new A/G Church in Wapuli when I complete NGBI.
> David Mankrom is in NGBI with me now and sends
> greetings.

Those two were serious about their call! Solomon K. Binambo
wrote about the wreck and said:

> Joshua Gewen Beso has gone back to Bawku to work.
> Edward Dondow, Timothy Binambil, and I work with
> Miss Smith.

I wrote my brother in Seattle:

> I have been in school six days and am six weeks behind.
> We have assignments that will take us that long to com-
> plete. Most of our science classes are taken in a building
> among beautiful pines in a hilly area. It is relaxing to
> drive there, but students need a car.

The nursing module we were to create was stimula-
tion for my analytical mind while someone else was call-

ing for an oral report. The book, *Future Shock*, was popular so I reported on the whole book in the time allotted. It is more relevant today, as each day passes. It reminded me of an actual situation when I once flew back from Africa. On a medication, a doctor's prescription read simply, "Take one tablet with breakfast." Well, we ate breakfast on a short stopover in Lisbon, Portugal; I took a pill. We flew west with the sun. They served us breakfast on the plane in mid-Atlantic; I took a pill. As we flew along with the sun and reached New York, the person who met me said, "We are taking you out for breakfast." Was I to take another pill with breakfast? That would be three within twelve hours instead of one in twenty-four hours! We are living in a faster world each day. I used an overhead projector to illustrate that all hospitals in the USA had changed their signs to read, *Stress Hospital*. In another illustration, I placed a punchboard on a wall outside a clinic door. It read, "We clone while you wait; punch choice of sex, color of eyes, color of hair, etc." Nearby at a poolside, a sign read, "Swim while you wait for your new baby." That was 1972! (As I write in the early 2000s, scientists are cloning body parts for transplant.) This course included teaching; we were allowed to use the media center. For practice teaching, we made our own 35mm slides, operated a video camera, and produced our own teaching material. Unknown to me, it was preparing me for my future in Nursing Education.

Nurses Joy King and Sharon Wallace sent me programs for the dedications of the new churches at Nakpanduri and Bunkpurugu in November. Eloise Smith went to Saboba and was enjoying the fruit of hard labor by the Konkombas, Ann Fisher, and me. I would go to Nakpanduri and enjoy the fruit of hard work by Joy King, Sharon Wallace, and the Bimobas. The Bimobas say, "It takes the hands of more than one man to reach around the baobob tree." Paul said in I Cor. 3:6, "I have planted, Apollos watered; but God gave the increase." Truly, let it be!

1. Johnstons see me off—1974. 2-3 Nakpanduri Clinic. 4. First MAPS nurse Cathy. 5. Beloved Deacon Elijah, Najong #2. 6. Nyankpen, from clinic helper to Bunkpurugu chief (wife, Waniib, 2-r in #8). 7-9. Wedding! Nakpanduri pastor John S. Yajen and Esther Nyankpen. #8. Party, L-R: teacher Andrew, Yajen, John and Esther, Eunice, bride's mom and another mom.

CHAPTER SEVEN

MAPS Nurses to the Rescue
Visitors from Kansas

A S IT TURNED OUT, Ann was my last fully appointed coworker for West Africa. She married Richard Bledsoe and I have kept aware of them and their two sons, Brian and Chris. I completed the Master of Nursing. That would contribute toward my retirement; I could care for myself after Africa. Ghana was changing fast. The Ghana Church was evolving to become indigenous. Even before Ann and I went to Saboba, Rev. Everett Phillips and I, jokingly, talked about indigenous clinics. He said, "This may be the way to go; the Executive Committee at Headquarters is talking along those lines."

However, there were at least two schools of thought on how this was to be accomplished. Some Mission Executives wanted to close the clinics. That seemed logical to them. The clinics had opened doors to establish churches in the Konkomba and Bimoba Tribes; the efforts were successful! The church became strong in those tribes, as nurses were busy and pastors took responsibilities. These areas soon had their own "Section and Presbyter." In doing this, the Assemblies of God had also contributed to the financial, educational, and physical well being of the people in both tribes. The people loved "their nurses." This love went both ways. Nurses, at one time, were, "trained in excellence." That meant that we could not see leaving the two tribes just the way we found them, with no medical facility within their borders. We wanted to "make them indigenous like the church." This meant getting locals trained to run the clinics like pastors were educated to direct the churches. Some mission executives agreed with the nurses, some disagreed. It was all relative to their vantage point. Some missionaries worked in cities where there were Government Hospitals and Clinics. Others worked in remote areas and understood the grave consequences of no medical facilities. The Ghana Government was not able, for reasons I am not politically savvy to follow, to provide medical aid in these remote areas. It provided our mission with the great opportunity to give health service and reach the people with the message of their path to God for eternity. That is the mandate of God's Word to His Church, "GO!" I felt Ann Fisher and I had a mandate from Everett Phillips before he retired, and from Morris Williams who followed him. We were to get *local* young Ghanaians, male and female, medically educated. The clinics must not close because American nurse practitioners and midwives were no longer available. Ann and I sent three young men into nursing programs from Saboba Clinic. Midwives Joy and Sharon sent one from Nakpanduri Clinic. That was a start!

ॐ ॐ ॐ

In June 1973, right after I completed the master's at "Ole Miss," I attended the wedding of John T. Goodwin and Amonna Sue McCorkle in Baytown, Texas. I had known them both as kids who called me Auntie in Africa. In September, I returned to Texas for the wedding of Ann Fisher and Richard Bledsoe in Lubbock, Texas. Ann had been my coworker, while Dick Bledsoe's brother and family were stationed across the Oti River from us in French Togo. I was speaking the 1/*nightly plus* 2/*Sunday* and packing for Africa. Since I had no coworker yet, I volunteered as Youth Camp nurse later in June. With more packing and speaking, the only rest I would have was Family Camp in July. Instead, I awoke one morning in my home in Albuquerque and my legs would not hold me up! Tests were done at Lovelace-Battaan Clinic. The white blood cell count and sedimentation rate were out of sight, abnormal! A possible diagnosis was the virulent Coxsackie virus. The prognosis: "It usually leaves (sterile) meningitis!"

By mid-August 1973 Huletta Gray, a teacher, and I rode with Pastor and Mrs. Northrop to Miami, Florida for the International Council of the Assemblies of God. Raymond H. Hudson, former District Superintendent in New Mexico, was elected General Treasurer. E.J. Namyela-Panka, Saboba First Assembly (Toma) Pastor and General Superintendent of Ghana Assemblies, was there as representative. He was a guest of the Franklin McCorkles. New Mexico District Officials invited them to visit our state. They accepted and I helped them itinerate in my area of New Mexico.

After months, Gideon Tadimie Jagir wrote from Ghana, "Dear Madam, it is a long time and I haven't heard. I was expecting to see you since long and I don't know why not. It may be you are no more coming and you don't want to tell us. Madam, how do you feel? Write me and I will write you about '*Saboba, your town.*'" John Kitinyaab wrote,"Had it not been for Miss Fisher, now Mrs. Dick, I could not even transmit a letter to you. I Peter 5:7." Then, Amos Biyimba, our faithful cook, had his daughter Ruthie write for him. "We heard you had no helper and were not feeling well. How is it?" I told someone, "I would give up, but how do you go about doing that?"

Because it became more difficult to find nurses and midwives for Ghana, we turned to the MAPS Department

(Mobilization and Placement Service) in our organization to provide temporary help. We found that our use of MAPS nurses was as controversial as ideas about the existence of medical clinics in Ghana. Again, both Everett Phillips and Morris Williams saw no other way to get American nurses. This solidified a dichotomy of opinions right down the middle, the clinic-friendly and the clinic-cynics. Morris Williams and I signed for MAPS nurses for both Saboba and Nakpanduri Clinics by date until the end of 1978. He mandated us to have Ghanaian midwives trained by then; we would certainly have Ghanaian male nurses by then.

I wrote my farewell letter to family and friends May 1974. New committee members in Ghana felt it best to keep the clinics open. I went ahead to Wichita to visit friends in churches and Wesley School of Nursing faculty. On our departure date, MAPS Nurse Cathy took a flight from Amarillo to Wichita. I quickly introduced her to my friends and joined her on a flight to New York. In England, we visited my Dalton friends in Bedford. I had asked Gretchen Lehmann Kast what to see in Switzerland, her husband's home. She drew maps for a trip from Zurich, Lucerne, Interlaken, and Jungfrau. It was Cathy's first trip overseas, so we saw as much as time allowed.

༕ ༕ ༕

We arrived in Ghana June 11, 1974. I knew not to predict arrival time of our freight. We drove north in a borrowed, open Land Rover for Cathy to see beautiful Ghana and meet missionaries. We were sent to Nakpanduri Clinic. I was resident missionary there for the first time since 1960, right after I was injured in the beating. At our welcome service in 1974, Pastor John Saban Yajen welcomed us and added, "I am not sure Madam Spencer knows that it was my father who ordered the kidnapping of the girl, her initiation into Kwansi, and the beating of the Christians. I was in primary school, but when I saw the miracles of how God protected the Christians, I chose to become a pastor."

The Bimobas who were beaten with me at Najong #2 were still there. I heard positive and negative reports about the girl we rescued. Because of her rescue, she was now free to choose her lifestyle. However, the rescue was not just about her; it was about all young Ghanaians forever. My right scapula had been broken and the clavicle dislocated, so E.J. Namyela-Panka had helped me shift gears in the Chevrolet back to the police station. Since then, he had been voted Northern District Superintendent and then General Superintendent of the Ghana Assemblies of God. In 1974, when Cathy and I got to Nakpanduri, he and his wife, Karen were still pastoring in Saboba but would soon move to an official residence in Tamale and have his own assigned vehicle. Pastors needed him near a phone; Saboba had none. Nyankpen, also beaten in the rescue in 1959, was my head clinic orderly then; I was his employer. Now, he was *Bimoba Chief Nyankpen Libagitib*, my superior!

The General Council of Ghana convened in Kumasi July 8-12. Cathy and I attended that and went on to Takoradi; our freight had arrived with our two STL vehicles, a car to save on fuel and a BIG red Chevrolet for an ambulance. We saw signs everywhere, "Move Right August 4." French Countries on three sides of Ghana always drove on the right. Cathy and I had said we wanted to be safely in Nakpanduri on August 4! Instead, we were in Accra, the capitol city, getting two vehicles licensed and insured. Ghanaian drivers were being cautious. Police were everywhere and few horns honked; it was a pleasure to drive! We drove the two vehicles north. We made a side trip from Tamale to visit Eloise Smith, her new coworker Mary Robbins, and the Konkombas in *"Saboba, my town."* Wow, what an emotional time!

Morris Williams wrote from Missouri:

Jean Webster, a fully appointed nurse, is ready to transfer from Liberia to Ghana. I have asked her to work with you. If there are adjustments, it must be on the part of the MAPS workers we requested. We are painfully aware that short-term nurses are not the way to run our program, but we seem to have no recourse just now.

Mission Officials in Ghana put Jean in Saboba to relieve Eloise Smith; she had already stayed an extra year! She left when Jean Webster (not a midwife) was oriented. The mission had signed to have "Midwifery Clinics." I was the only mission midwife in Ghana, so Chairman of the Clinic Committee, Franklin McCorkle, declared me Matron of all our clinics to keep them legal. He wrote, "In spite of your busy schedule, please communicate with Ghana Medical Officials to keep a Ghanaian midwife in Saboba with Jean." Some naive souls thought I, instead of the mission officials, was to solve housekeeping and moral or dress code problems! I was not to run Saboba Clinic, only to allow my credentials to keep the mission legal "to save the ranch!" A Mission Chairman, Vernon Driggers, once wrote to headquarters in Missouri:

> We cannot stress too strongly the importance this present government places on social work such as clinics. Yet, a nurse needs a call from God to go to remote clinics to stay for years!

How true!

On September 10, 1974, Pastor of the Nakpanduri Church, John Saban Yajen, married Esther N. Libagitib, daughter of the Bimoba Chief at Bunkpurugu. Yajen, Pastor John's father, came from Najong #2 for the wedding. (One August day at Najong #2, Yajen, father of this groom had ordered the beating, with intent to kill, of the father of this bride! Since then, the once-beaten father of the bride had become chief over an area that included Yajen's village.) Shortly after Pastor John's' wedding, he entered the West African Advanced School of Theology (WAAST) in Lome, Togo. While he was gone, we hired his wife, Esther, to work in the clinic as her father, the present Chief at Bunkpurugu, once had done. She was good with mothers and children.

Presbyter Yakubu Kujar pastored the Bimbagu church and chaired monthly pastors' meetings; he would soon be going to WAAST also. At one such meeting, I reported to them about a gift from Pastor and Mrs. R.C. Dobyns at Calvary Assembly in Albuquerque. They and a group called *Christ for the Nations* gave money for a much-needed new church in Pakinatiik. The building process started! I reported my need to build a watchman's quarters at our residence gate. I felt we were too isolated to have the young MAPS nurse without a responsible Ghanaian nearby; more young nurses were coming. The pastors planned for two conventions each year. One at Easter was for evangelism. Lives were changed and new groups established. A church must be ready for the next new pastor graduating from N. Ghana Bible School. The New Year's Convention allowed new Christians to observe the operation of the gifts of the Holy Spirit within the church. Results were positive and instant. A fetish priestess gave her animated testimony of how God delivered her from idol worship.

Yes, Ghana was changing! One day we drove on the left, next day on the right. One day we were told that we had less than a week to change our money for a percentage of new money at the bank. Pastors collected money from people who had no transportation and kept books. We drove one hundred twenty miles to Tamale, had it changed, and returned it to owners. The price of everything doubled in a short time. This prompted a letter from our Division of Foreign Missions. "Future operations of clinics depend on availability of finance. Usually, the clinic is underwritten through the nurse who cares for it." I was that nurse! I wrote home and people responded, as usual.

Cathy left when her year was up. We drove to Accra to meet her plane and to get Claudia, her MAPS replacement from Virginia. Kathy eventually sent an announcement of her wedding. H. "Spud" DeMent, Representative of MAPS in the USA wrote me, "We are proud of you and interested in helping any way we can. The schedule you planned with Morris Williams is working!" I replied, "The Bimobas are grateful you sent Cathy. She worked hard. For pleasure, we made one trip to Mole Game Reserve and one to Upper Volta."

My June 1975 newsletter to family, friends, and donors in America was about our clinic workers and their families. They were 1) Paul Jatuat Sillim, son of the Nakpanduri Chief, interpreter, and medication dispenser; 2) Awuni Dubik, a local church elder with the clinic since the 1950s. He helps with maternity cases any time day or night. We are hoping his eldest daughter goes for midwifery training. 3) Esther Nyankpen Saban-Yajen works to support herself and we can let her husband in WAAST know how she is! 4) Peter Lari, married with children, is our only professionally trained Ghanaian nurse. Joy and Sharon sent him for schooling. 5) Samson Bumbommong, married with a *new* baby, is file clerk. 6) Joseph Kombet, a file clerk from Najong #2, is saving to go to Bible College.

The new MAPS Nurse and I made a trip to Ouagadougou for items we could not buy in Ghana. Many years it was the other way around; they came to Ghana. On the way back we were hopelessly stuck in a sand bar and a lion stalked us all night. Men coming by the next morning got our car out of the sand. I had a policy never to travel without a Ghanaian! *And did I learn anything?* It taught me to stick to my policy!

༄ ༄ ༄

Dedication of the new Pakinatiik Church took place December 11, 1975. The youth group in an Albuquerque church drew posters and put them on their walls to help raise the money, then gave them to me. At the new church dedication, we unrolled the posters and stretched them on the walls. The pastor at Pakinatiik was a recent graduate of Northern Ghana Bible Institute, so Teacher Peter Yamusah, from NGBI, came and married Pastor Natuka and Elizabeth during the dedication. They moved into a new parsonage built by members of the church while the church was being built. A year later, Pastor and Elizabeth had a child. Pastor Moses Natuka declared the whole scenario a one-year record: new graduate pastor, new church, new wife, and new baby!

ↄ ↄ ↄ

Christmas was another real celebration! After a service inside the church, they went outside. A 45-gallon drum of hot tea with sugar and canned milk brewed on a bonfire. While circling the fire in rhythm, they sang every carol and worship chorus they knew and made some up as they went. I often moved away from the fire, sat quietly on a log, and watched satellites slide across the starry sky. We usually had a party for our workers and their families. Lights were strung in the trees. Inside we had an artificial tree with lights and a tape of carols playing. Israel, Nurse Peter's son, ran to his father and declared, "My Father, there is a tree in there and it's singing!"

On January 1976, a letter came from Ruth Biyimba in Midwifery training. She wrote:

> I am so very happy to get the chance of coming to this school. We started duty on the wards today! We have tests for the next two weeks; remember me in prayer. I don't know just how to thank you, but God bless you forever.
>
> Your beloved, Ruth Biyimba

A letter from a daughter of Amos Biyimba was all the thanks I ever needed. With a yaws-eaten body at age 11, he was not supposed to be alive, much less have a daughter aiming at a nurse-midwife career.

On a Saturday afternoon, we went to Tambien to help pastors in an evangelistic effort. They even slept there while visiting in every home. Already twenty-one people had accepted God's Son as their sacrifice. That evening, fifteen more joined the group. A church was born, the second that month. They were *footing it* with this kind of results. It prompted me to write for three bicycles. Pastor C. Eddie Lee, Youth and Education Director in New Mexico, answered:

> I am glad we can be of help with bicycles for evangelism. My heart thrills at these efforts along with your clinic work. We appreciate your taking our place to reach Africa with the Gospel of Jesus Christ.

At the next pastors' meeting, they decided how and where the three Raleigh bicycles were to be used. New and larger churches were needed and in the process of being built at Najong #1 and Gbankoni. First mud churches were going up at Tambien and Nasuan.

I prepared a clinic report for the Clinic Committee Meeting in February 1976 and the Annual Missionary Convention. We had treated 20,576 cases, an average of 1,700 per month. All this was possible because we had good Ghanaian help at clinic and house. Emmanuel Billin was cook, laundryman, and housekeeper. Like Biyimba at Saboba, he managed our house! He and Hannah lived in our newly completed watchman's quarters. They had no child until Paulina was born. We nursed Hannah through a rough pre-eclamptic pregnancy, as she lived right at our gate.

A young man, Issifu Sillim, helped Emmanuel but hated housework. One day he saw our yardman, Kombat, tilling with a short handled hoe. He got his father's plow and ox and tilled our garden plot free! When we transported him to Bawku Technical Institute, he was happy; no more housework! He advanced from caring for a dignitary's car, to instructor in a technical school. He wrote, "You would be impressed at my salary!" I could not pay him much to dust furniture! A young man named Isaac replaced Issifu in our watchman's quarters and helped Emmanuel at our house and us at the clinic.

As long as Franklin McCorkle was Chairman of the Clinic Committee, we experienced fairness. Jean Webster, the nurse who transferred from Liberia, was due for furlough in 1977 and so was I. At one such committee meeting, Franklin asked me to go home to the USA when my MAPS coworker, Claudia went, take a mini-furlough of four months, and come back for two more years with two more MAPS nurses that were already scheduled. I was to ask Ghana Medical Officials for a loan of a Ghanaian midwife for Nakpanduri for those four months. I followed through with a request.

As long as John L. Weidman was "Secretary, *the people's choice,*" of the Clinic Committee, the most serious business would be punctuated with humor, verbally and in writing! He noted one member absent because of "malaria in the area." He recorded that the present MAPS nurse should *go get her midwifery* and, "Come back and HEP us!"

On our return trip, we picked up our mail in Gambaga. A prophetic letter had come from a Kay McGhee, in Louisiana. She saw an article I had written for the *Evangel* in April 1975, *More Than Nursing*. She told her pastor, David Savage, she felt I needed prayer. He said he knew me in New Mexico and that his Aunt Betty Savage was a missionary to Africa. Mrs. McGhee wrote me the words of a song, "I shall not be; I shall not be moved. Just like a tree that's planted by the water, I shall not be moved." A similar letter came when I was beaten at Najong #2. WOW! It left me wondering what was to come!

The clinic had to be stocked with medications for the four months I would be gone. It was decided Paul Jatuat Sillim, the chief's son, would go with me to Accra. MAPS Nurse Claudia stayed to supervise the clinic. Jatuat and I drove through the beautiful Ashanti Forest hill country to Kumasi. A man recommended we go straight south to Takoradi and then east to Accra, the capitol. I had never traveled that way. We soon met a two-rut diversion (detour). It took us under a canopy of tropical foliage for miles; we turned on the lorry (vehicle) lights. Paul Jatuat even asked if I thought this was the right way. Suddenly we came out into the light!

In Takoradi, we saw a huge ship docked in the harbor. We waded in the Gulf of Guinea. At Saltpond, we visited with students at Southern Ghana Bible Institute (SGBI). In Accra, we shopped in Kingsway Stores and at pharmaceutical companies. By the time we left, Paul Jatuat knew Accra quite well! We took a more direct route north through Koforidua back to Kumasi. On a mountainous road north of Kumasi, we came upon a serious lorry accident where Paul Jatuat said, "Oh, Madam, this is wonderful!" I could never get ready for that word to mean both negative and positive, but he was correct; it was *full of wonder!* We were asked to go ahead to inform the police at Mampong. We met the police and they knew, so we rushed on north to Nakpanduri and work.

There was one more Clinic Board Meeting at Kumbungu on May 13, before the second MAPS Nurse and I departed for America. Two more members were present this time; the one with malaria had survived. Rev. Panada Azong, Northern Ghana Superintendent was there to observe until a change in bylaws could legalize it at a Mission Conference. The Ghanaians wanted to be aware of the status of the clinics. John Weidman's minutes read, "Despite our four hundred-mile trek into the North, the anticipated snow storm did not materialize, evident by sweat on the agenda and minutes." I reported to the Clinic Committee that Midwife Susanna Musah had been found to fill in at Nakpanduri while I was on the mini-furlough. Nurse Jean Webster had hired Nurse Joel Ubor Wumbei to help in Saboba Clinic. Ann Fisher and I had sent Joel to Bawku Hospital for nurse's training when we were at Saboba. As a student nurse, he always ended his letters to us, "Oh, when will we meet and laugh again?"

Since there would be no mission nurse to do village child welfare clinics in my four-month absence, they recommended we purchase a Honda 125 so Nurse Peter could reach them. Jean Webster, at Saboba, could use the Big Red pickup and my car would be stored with the field Chairman in Kumasi. The next Clinic Committee Meeting was announced for November 11, 1976, after I returned from my short furlough. Mary Ann Vespa prepared a meal, which was a farewell for MAPS Nurse Claudia and me.

When the time came, we drove to Tamale where we left the pickup for Jean to use. We drove to Kumasi, left my car, and flew to Accra. It was too late to send flight plans to families; we would arrive there first. (Obviously, e-mail was not available yet!) On May 22, we flew Alatalia Airline to Rome. At The Hague, we visited Kansas friends Rev. and Mrs. David Richards, Sandi Lowenberg, and Brenda Benagis. We flew Pan American Airways from Frankfort, Germany to New York where Claudia and I parted. I flew to Springfield, Missouri, where I stayed with the Hudsons again. From there I phoned home and received the news that Mamaw Layman, my maternal grandmother, had died at age 91 on May 30 while we were in transit; I missed the funeral.

I made a quick stop in Kansas where the Paul Lowenbergs alerted me that they would visit Africa, including Ghana, in October. Back in Springfield, the School of Missions met June 7-8 with the theme of, "Facing the Winds of Change! Hebrews 18:8." Then I rode with Elaine Borne to Louisiana to fulfill a promise made to Mary Gray Waldon to speak for their WMs at the Louisiana District Council on June 23. I planned to visit Bill and Gale Dunning in Pawhuska, Oklahoma on my way to New Mexico and perhaps speak at their church; she was Mom's cousin. This plan was cut short by another death message. My very dear Uncle John, Dad's brother, had died. I flew to New Mexico for that funeral.

In mid-July, I attended a week of New Mexico Family Camp in Mountainair, New Mexico (Gateway to ancient cities and my birthplace). Near the end of camp, MAPS Nurse Claudia and her parents arrived from Virginia. I took them on a short trip south to Gran Quivira Indian Ruins. We might see a cattle drive with real cowboys! We actually saw one man on horseback and a rabbit ran across the road. So much for the *Wild, Wild West!* I shared Ghana news with Claudia. Ruth Biyimba had written, "Thank God with me for I was successful in my probation exams." A future midwife for Ghana clinics! Before I knew it, two of my four months of furlough were gone. I sent a cablegram to Ghana General Council that ended, "See you in October with another MAPS nurse!" How little I knew!

People tried to help me, because they knew my furlough was short. I hated motels; they ate up money I could use to roof a church! Sometimes I stayed in guestrooms in pastors' homes. I've been a guest of Doris Stewart, a niece of Marie Hudson, in Hobbs. James and Mary Lou Otts allowed me to stay in their Carlsbad home as needed. At least three families in First Assembly had airplanes, the Jacksons, the Kelleys, and the Otts. They all helped speed up my itinerary of *1/nightly and 2/Sundays*. When Mr. Jackson had business in Midland, Texas, I went along to visit Ann and Dick Bledsoe. James flew me to El Paso, where I presented my Africa plans at a church pastored by the John Hutson family. I knew them from SAGU in Waxahachie, Texas. From El Paso, I took a commercial round-trip flight to San Diego. On a stopover in Phoenix, I visited my Aunt Leonora and family, the Bill and Mae Cohea family, and others from former employment and in churches. In Southern California, I visited Mae and Dave Lynch and my three nephews. They taxied me to visit Fred and Bonnie Chambers, Cecil and Lois Holley, and other friends formerly of New Mexico. Back in El Paso, I paid my respects to Aunt Dode Layman. Uncle Jack Layman, Mom's brother, had died during my last term in Ghana. On Saturday, James Otts flew me back to Carlsbad.

Along the way to TorC to visit my parents, I spoke in different churches about the medical work in Africa and the results. One town was Anthony, where Willis and Ann Deerman were pastoring. My membership was in Central Assembly where G.B. Manning pastored; it was the nearest church to my house in Albuquerque. Pastor and Mrs. Dobyns of Calvary Assembly in Albuquerque, helped finance the Pakinatiik Church we built and dedicated. While I was saying thank you to these churches, I noticed how unusually painful it was to carry the 16mm movie projector and set up my equipment. I was sweating unnaturally; *something was amiss!* I took overseas shots as I packed for my fifth trip to Africa. I was allowed to pack in the WMs Room where Rowena Vanzant had her District Office. Mrs. Beunah Chaney, my Mom from TorC and Betty Olsen from Denver, helped me pack. Betty lodged with Chaneys (Secretary-Treasure of NMDC), as I had rented my house to Danny and Roxanne Piatt and their two daughters, Erin Michelle and Hannah Marie (who was born there). Roxanne is my niece that still calls me Auntie Who." Danny was attending UNM; I felt I was helping young people in their education on both sides of the ocean.

My mail was being collected at the NM District Council Offices in Albuquerque. One was from Lamar Headley, Representative of MAPS, who wrote, "We have sent Carol and Dian the necessary requirements to obtain a visa for Ghana. If for any reason you feel you cannot use Dian at Saboba and Carol at Nakpanduri as planned, let us know." I phoned them both. There was no way Carol would be ready to go with me to Nakpanduri Clinic as the Ghana Committee hoped.

On September 14, I sent out a "TO GHANA, BYE-BYE" letter and went east. I had a service with the Dunning's in Oklahoma, where I had previously rushed away to a funeral. In Springfield, Missouri, I bade farewell to Raymond and

Marie Hudson. They deserve my reward in Heaven for cars they have loaned me! There, I was asked to make a side trip to Kansas City for a Citywide 1976 Missions Convention. We were told where to speak. John Garlock was one of the speakers. His father, Henry Garlock, held the position in 1953 that Morris Williams held in 1976. I told John Garlock a Saboba story: "In 1954 our Saboba Clinic helper, Gylima Akonsi, son of the *first Konkomba Christian*, told me the Garlock children were the first white children they ever saw. Gylima said, 'Before that, we thought white people came out of the sea like the fish up the Oti River!'"

On a layover near Nashville, Tennessee, I spoke in the church of my former TorC pastors, Carl and Jewel Walker. Then, at Dulles Airport outside Washington, DC, MAPS Nurse Claudia and her parents drove from Nokesville, Virginia to meet my plane. They insisted I go to a doctor as I was having trouble walking. He did minor surgery on my right foot and applied such a huge bandage that TWA Officials required a doctor's permit for me to fly to Philadelphia. There I met Ruth Whitecap, a missionary to Spain from Lancaster, Pennsylvania, Helen Kopp's hometown. I joined her flight to London. We shared a room at the Cumberland Hotel. The 11th Pentecostal World Conference was in progress at London's Royal Albert Hall. Ruth attended; I did not. I was there to order the two Lister diesel generators for the clinics; they were less expensive directly from London. My foot hurt even as I took subway tubes to sales houses around cold, wet London. The Division of Foreign Missions in Missouri wired money to pay for the generators and freight to Ghana.

Ruth and I flew by Sabena Airline to Brussels, Belgium. We visited people and places she was familiar with. I was familiar with names like Walker, Jester, and Flattery at the International Bible School and Correspondence School. With that bit of rest, my foot improved. However, on that whole journey, I kept feeling heat in my back against the backs of airplane seats. I thought they had put heaters in the backs of the seats to conserve space in overseas flights. I have come to know it was my spinal cord inside the bony canal, the meninges (cord, brain, and nerve coverings) and nerves going out from the spinal cord were that hot!

On Tuesday, October 5, we flew to Spain via Iberian Airlines. We spent one day in Madrid and one at Avila, a magnificent old walled city. Ruth lived in Barcelona, but was soon moving to Tenerife in the Spanish Canary Islands. On Friday, October 8, I flew Swiss-Air to Zurich where I had a two-hour wait before the same airline flew me to Ghana for my fifth term. What a grand surprise met me at Accra Airport! Paul Jatuat, the Nakpanduri Clinic worker, was there along with Missionary Krakes and others. Jatuat had come by lorry transport over five hundred miles! He had traveled south with me earlier, so he knew Accra. He brought a list of medications and supplies needed at the clinic. The Driggers had my car serviced in Kumasi and drove it to Accra. Jatuat and I spent two days shopping in Accra and headed north. I was not forced to travel alone! Over a meal in Kumasi, I thanked the Driggers for caring for my car. First, Jatuat and I talked about the bad lorry accident we once saw on those same Ashanti Hills. That caused us to think of the diversion we once took through a dense jungle. Jatuat said, "It was so dark under the tall trees and the road went on and on. In fact, Madam, I thought we were missing!" Here was another use of the English language that described the situation exactly, but surprised me! Either we might have been *missing the road* or *we, ourselves, could have been missing forever*!

The McCorkles were still at NGBI in Kumbungu; we stopped to greet them. I was going to be alone until a MAPS nurse arrived, so they gave me an all-black male pup of their dog, Ginger; I named him Ebony. A half-Rhodesian Ridgeback and half-black Labrador retriever belonging to the Pong Tamale Vet had sired the pups. Ebony's body shape was Alsatian, his muzzle was broad like a Lab, and a ridge stood up the full length of his back. At the Tamale Post Office, Paul Jatuat helped load sacks of mail; postal workers were on strike. In Gambaga, we waited for ours. We entered Nakpanduri to a rousing din of, "Welcome, Madam!" by villagers, pastors, clinic workers, and the borrowed midwife. Emmanuel Billin had my house clean and waiting! In the mail was a letter from Superintendent Earl Vanzant, in Albuquerque. He said vandals had set fire inside their office building where I packed! My leftover things had not yet been moved to the third bedroom of my house that I kept locked for storage; there had been no hurry! Within days, I took Midwife Susana Musah to Tamale and wrote a letter of thanks to Dr. Darkwa and Miss Lamptey for their loan.

I had to drive Big Red quite a lot when I first got back to Ghana. One day, I was driving to NGBI at Kumbungu when the clutch plate slid to a stop! For the first time in Africa, I had to have a vehicle towed twenty miles for repair in Tamale. The missionary men, who had always bragged on my road-worthy vehicles, had a heyday teasing me! The clutch was repaired; Big Red was on the road again. A doctor ordered me to bed for two weeks with my foot on a pillow because of *cellulitis*. Pauline Smith and Adeline Wichmann, returning from furlough, borrowed Big Red to haul freight. They complained about a stiff clutch; I fully agreed!

With a pickup repaired just in time, we met Rev. Paul and Bernice Lowenberg from Kansas on October 26. Seven Bimoba pastors proudly accompanied me to the Tamale Airport to meet them in Speed-the-Light's big red Chevrolet. We spent the night at NGBI where Rev. Lowenberg spoke twice in chapel to faculty, students, and national ministers. On the eleven-mile trek to Tamale, a tire went flat. Ten of us easily put on the spare, but I vented my frustration at not having a spare for the rest of the three hundred-mile journey. Paul Lowenberg said, "Don't worry, Charlese, when we get to Tamale we will buy you a new tire." I knew it would be a miracle if a tire the right size existed in all Ghana! My freight with the new set had not arrived from the mini-furlough. We found one that fit the rim, but the radius was smaller than others on the pickup were. We had it prepared as a spare, and drove on the one hundred miles through Yendi to Saboba. Ruby Johnson was from Kansas, she and Ozella Reid Hager were the first nurses at Saboba in 1949. The Lowenbergs must meet Ruby's beloved Konkombas! From Yendi, we chose the road through Demon to Saboba. Our first stop was Kokonzoli, the church built when Ann Fisher and I were in Saboba. Our next stop was Saboba, where Jean Webster was alone. The people welcomed the Americans and Bimoba pastors royally! They demanded firsthand news from Ruby Johnson and all American nurses.

The flat tire and mud had slowed our progress, so we spent the night as guests of Jean. The next morning we drove through Wapuli, where the God-called Emmanuel Gundow Wumbei family pastored. The rains lasted late that year, so Pastor Emmanuel waded water about two miles to show us the road to Yankazia; we followed in the pickup. The Lowenbergs started saying, "Charlese, you surely do live dangerously!" I do try hard; I believe people are that important to God! Pastor Samson Abarika and family, U Na Fabor Jayum, and the villagers were waiting in another church built while Ann and I lived in Saboba. It was an emotional reunion and probably the last time I saw the beloved Christian Chief of Yankazia. Pastor Emmanuel led us back as he had led us in. We drove three hours north to Nakpanduri Clinic on the unpaved Gushiago moto'way.

1.Major intersection, round-about in Nakpanduri and an outstation road. 2. Rev. Simon J. Masak and Eunice Samson wedding by Presbyter Sulemana. 3. Pastor Jeremiah Y. Kombet weds Mahatabel, biggest one yet. 4. STL crossing Volta Lake, former river! And moving to right side of the road Aug. 4, 1974. 5. Lay pastor Samson and helpers begin a new Najong #1 church. 6. Good helpers at house move into new watchman's quarters. 7-8 Second MAPS nurse registers at American Embassy, Accra. 9. Ginger and Biyenoqua.

1. Furlough travel 1976 (meni-) 2-4 packing at NMDC, Mom, B. Chaney and B. Olsen from Denver. Shipping to Houston Port, Darrald Ray and Royce R. 5. Dad at Brother John's funeral. 6. Kansas visitors, Rev. Paul and Mrs. Lowenberg. 7-8. 1977 New Year's convention. With sign: Isifu Sillim and Peter Bandim. Eleven Bimoba pastors, congregation and speakers: Rev. and Mrs. (Karen) E.J. Namyela Panka, Gen. Supt. Of Ghana A/G. 9. Pres. Y. Kujar and pastors Simon J. and Jeremiah receiving gifts from USA churches. 10. Esther (Nyankpen) Yajen, clinic child welfare worker.

1. Pastors away for higher education. 2. MAPS nurses: 1st: Diane; 2nd: Carol; 3rd: Holly (after my mini-furlough) … with our house and clinic workers and wives and new born babies. 3. Pastors and their wives and families. 4. Transporting pastors to district councils etc.; wives to retreats; and young people to camps. (L.L.: another #2 "Joanna.")

Chapter Eight

Miracles and More MAPS Nurses
New King; New Law

THE LOWENBERGS ONLY STAYED overnight in Nakpanduri. The next morning, they observed the clinic in operation. I took them on the mandatory trip to the escarpment at the north edge Nakpanduri. From the top, you could see the Bawku Mountain forty miles away. It was market day; people walked up as we drove almost straight down the half-mile to a branch of the Volta River. It was helping to form the new Volta Lake. Mothers, with babies cuddled on their backs, had wares to sell balanced on their heads. That afternoon, I drove the Lowenbergs sixty miles south to Walewale, where we met Curtis Dean, a Kansas missionary. He transported them to Upper Volta (now Burkina Faso).

Eventually, the Lowenbergs mailed us the report of their tour of Europe and West Africa. It sounded like a Who's Who of Kansas: Sam and Joyce Johnson in Spain; the Lowenbergs' own daughter, Sandi, with Brenda Benigas and the David Richards in Holland; Big Bob and Bonnie Mackish in Austria and Czechoslovakia; Al Pernas in Rome where *"traffic was like spaghetti and a miss as good as a mile."* Marge and Roger Metz in Nigeria had introduced them to Africa. WAAST

Faculty, in Lome, Togo was loaded with Kansans: Rex and Martha Jackson and Bill and Peggy (Jones) Lasley for starters. (Later, in 2002-3, their own Doug Lowenberg and family would be on that WAAST Faculty.) Their Ghana visit was before Upper Volta, then Senegal with Ernest, Marge and Jan Jones, and finally Laura Musgrove in Belgium at ICI.

After their visit to Nakpanduri, I realized my hands and feet were getting more spastic; my back was getting hotter. At a Pastors' meeting, I told the men, "The area is requiring more strength than I have to offer." Some apologized. Issifu, who once tilled my garden plot with his father's plow and ox, wrote from Bawku Technical School, "I think of how you are going to manage to take every emergency to Nalerigu Hospital, since you have come back to Ghana alone. I think until I am tired and fall asleep; the next night I continue thinking. If you teach me to drive, I can help transport emergencies when I'm on break." I thought this delightful student was learning automobile mechanics; it was sounding more like civil engineering! Gideon N. Panka was a student in Secondary School in Bawku. He was such a good student that, on my visits, the Head Master would proudly show me his name on a bulletin board for having excelled somehow.

In late November 1976, a note came from a man in Najong #2, "I want to go to Kumbungu and see my son, James, graduate from NGBI." Mercy, that smacked of *déjà vu*, I had no coworker and was going to Najong #2 with pastors! At the village, the man climbed into the cab between a pastor and me. I once identified the man in court as breaking my nose at my Kingswood Chevrolet car door! I had heard that one of those who beat us became Superintendent of Sunday School in his local church. This was the man and his son was graduating to be a pastor--another miracle! (In January 2003, I was notified when he died. I found myself in mourning for the man who injured me!)

Immediately after the NGBI Graduation, we drove south and east to the West African Advanced School of Theology

Graduation at Lome, Togo. Our Bimoba Presbyter, Yakubu Sokpam Kujar, was graduating. Maynard Ketcham from the USA was speaker. Other Ghanaians, John Saban Yajen, Simon Asore, Joseph Mills, and Joseph Mensah would graduate within the next two years. We returned at once to Accra, Ghana, where I became ill with a high fever; I always assumed it was malaria. Someone drove Big Red north to transport our students; I followed later by plane.

The Bimoba Section New Year's Convention, December 31 to January 3, 1977, was held at Pakinatiik, the newest church dedicated. They added an arbor for the big event! The Host Pastor was Moses Natuka; Rev. Timothy Kere was guest speaker. Pastor Simon J. Masak was interpreter for English and Mwor. Pastor John Kombat led prayer and worship. (When Elder Lamboan broke my nose at my car door, he took my keys to the local Chief Masak, Simon's father. He held the keys as Pastor John Kombat and others were beaten.) Pastors Simon and John, leaders in this 1977 convention, reminded us again of the many miracles! There was more than one minister from Najong #2 for every Christian beaten! Since I was still alone, the W.F. McCorkles came from Walewale for that convention. We commuted nightly to sleep in Nakpanduri; the Ghanaians lodged in local homes in Pakinatiik.

After the convention, John Saban was returning to WAAST in Lome, Togo for his last year, Presbyter Thompson Tonlaar for his first year. I took them as far as Accra, as the generators I purchased in London had arrived by ship. The students continued to Lome by other means of transport. Financial aid came for them from many sources, perhaps a previous pastorate or even MAPS Nurses. I kept books. When they were not allowed to pay in Ghana Cedis, I asked for an explanation from President Rex Jackson and the students. Finally, T. Tonlaar wrote:

> I told you how I had to work to pay the balance, so I could receive my grades. Then you wrote, asking again!

How can I explain again? My people say, 'A male donkey does not bray (make a scene) in his friends' compound.' Here, they say we pay dollars or francs! If we do not, it is not their lookout; they send us home! We are ending second trimester and I have not paid for a single textbook. They are so costly, you can never understand!

We sent dollars!

While in Accra, I learned that Jeanette Boteler, a nurse under full appointment, was transferring from Nigeria to Ghana. Too bad, she was not a midwife! I was familiar with that name in New Mexico; I had met her as a child. She did arrive and her STL vehicle would follow by ship. She flew straight to Tamale in time for Northern Ghana District Council at Kumbungu. She could work with Jean Webster in Saboba and replace Jean at furlough-time in three months.

I drove Big Red north to Kumasi, had foot surgery as scheduled on January 25 with Dr. Bowesman; I have his book *Surgery in the Tropics*. I stayed in the guesthouse of Ashanti Area Supervisors Vernon and Maxine Driggers. A letter arrived from Nurse Peter Lari, at Nakpanduri Clinic:

> We had two hundred sixty-three at the well baby clinic in Nakpanduri this week. Since you left, we took in enough to pay all helpers at the end of January; I hope it was not wrong to pay them. I beg you to rest and get well! OK? We are praying for you and *working hard*.

He knew both would impress me!

MAPS Nurse Diane, scheduled for Saboba Clinic, arrived in Accra just after I went to Kumasi. She flew north to Kumasi, where I was having the surgery. When I could travel, Diane drove us north to Tamale in Big Red and on to NGBI for Northern Ghana District Council at Kumbungu. Diane was an excellent driver, an answer to prayer! There, we met Nurse Jeanette Boteler. With the new surgery and a fall that sprained my back, I did not attend one session of District Council. I had typed Presbyter Tonlaar's Sectional

Report before he went to WAAST. Pastor Yakubu Kujar, read it at District Council. It read:

> ... God has multiplied the number of Bimoba Pastors! Three recent graduates make fourteen. Pastor Jeremiah Kombat is pastoring in Nakpanduri as John Saban Yajen went to WAAST for an advanced degree. New graduates are pastoring as follows: Joseph Junjong at Najong #2, Edward Toatir at Nasuan, and James Lamboan at Kombatiak. There are nine mature, well-organized churches in the area. The new building at Pakinatiik has been dedicated. At Konchian Gberouk, over fifty people meet on Sundays; at Bombil, twenty-six have taken the new converts' course and are ready for baptism and membership. Larger churches are being built at Najong #1 and Gbankoni. Mud churches (beginners) will soon be built at Bombil, Nasuan, and Gberouk. By tithing on our building funds, we are financing the District Council to plant churches in the Western Region of Ghana. Pray for our Area Supervisor, Miss Spencer; the clinic and area are difficult for one. Brother Yakubu, a graduate from WAAST, has agreed to present this. Brother John S. Yajen is in his last year at WAAST. He and I will return to work in the Bimoba Section.

> Respectfully submitted,
> Thompson Tonlaar, WAAST

In 1978, Berniece Lowenberg of Wichita, Kansas wrote:

> The work of Charlese at the Nakpanduri Clinic would make an exciting book, another chapter in the book of Acts. We were there two years ago, and saw the results first-hand. We talked with the chief of the tribe who was beaten when she was. He said, "Miss Spencer is like my right arm; I do not know what my people would do without her help." We saw the churches that were started through the ministry of the clinics. We saw

many churches they built by hauling sand, lumber, and water between clinic sessions. We saw the thousands of patients she treated and gave food to every week. She had no co-worker yet, but had trained Ghanaians to help. At Gospel services, people heard a message from the Word before they received healing from her kind hands. We saw babies she had delivered in the early hours before or after a grueling day at the clinic and at building sites. The mission house she lived in was broken down, as you can't repair a mission house and look after a thousand people a week (or day) at the same time. What a triumph for the Gospel and the Assemblies of God in that part of Africa!

(Permission to use this letter was given by her husband, Rev. Paul Lowenberg, as she went to be with her Lord-Jesus Sept. 28, 1998. She wrote this to the DFM at headquarters to ask how the Kansas WMs could support an American nurse going to the Nakpanduri clinic after I left.)

In Dec. 1978, from Wichita, KS (to me):

A telecast was appealing for nurses to teach in Oral Roberts University. You would not be so far from us and could come to see us. Do you think I have a motive? Our children will be home for Christmas.

Sandi is going with a young man. Doug is busy serving the Lord and going with no one; he loves them all. Brother Lowe has been speaking from New York to Louisiana; we now fly instead of driving.

Sandi married the young man, James Bradford, and they have Meredith and Angeline Kallyce. The Lowenberg grandparents say they have red hair. Doug married Corrine and in September 1988 he wrote from Ouagadougou, Burkina Faso (Upper Volta), Sept. 1988, "We are not far from your ole stomping grounds. We preach, pray, and testify in Moore." Their Julia was with them in West Africa; Ruth Ann was born back in the USA. (Later, Doug and his family went

to Ethiopia under full appointment, then to Togo at WAAST
and Kenya in 2005 to set up a doctorate program.) I still see
to be Aunt Charlese to all.

It was decided that MAPS Nurse Diane should go with
me to Nakpanduri until the scheduled MAPS Nurse Carol
arrived. Jeanette Boteler, under full appointment, would
join Jean Webster, under full appointment, in Saboba. Neither were midwives, so I was mandated to keep a Ghanaian
midwife there. Diane was disappointed and made a quick
trip to see Saboba and get her mail. She wrote later, "Now
I'm in Nakpanduri and liking it; there are pythons instead
of cobras. YUK!" MAPS Nurse Carol did arrive in February.
While there were three of us, I got the rest I needed for my
foot. In addition, we sent out a regular letter to the Bimoba
boarding school students.

Peter Bandim of Nakpanduri replied, "Hello, it's me,
Peter, who has kept you anxiously waiting for a letter. I am
subjected to too much pressure by books, so please exercise
patience." His self-esteem was intact! Isaac Bandim wrote,
"Our school comes to an end 25th of March; will there be an
Easter Convention?" School breaks usually allowed boarding students to be with us for the two conventions per year.
Issifu Sillim wrote complaining that school fees had doubled
and he had worked for me on leave, but I had not taught him
to drive.

Ghana Local Councils provided all school fees, but higher
fees made space more competitive; they had to work harder.
Konkomba boarding students, from Saboba area, saw our
letter to Bimoba students and wrote us. I heard from Peter
and John, who had completed IPT in Kumasi. Peter was in
Tamale, hired by the Ghana Cotton Board. He wrote, "John
marched in a big parade in Accra; he has asked for your
address." John wrote, "I have entered the Ghana Armed
Forces for electrical engineering. Madams, do not relax your
prayers for me." (I am reminded of how concerned he was
in Kumasi IPT when heads were being collected for celebrat-

ing an anniversary of a chief's death. Here he was asking for prayer again.) Gideon N. Panka wrote again from Bawku Secondary School, "I attended Northern Ghana Youth Camp on leave, and carried its' Kingship home with pride to my parents in Tamale. Hannah Biyimba was Queen." She was our famous Saboba cook's daughter who happily cared for one twin brother while her grateful mother cared for the other.

Jeanette complained to someone about difficult and dirty living conditions at Saboba. Ruby and I often said this would happen when younger nurses, who had coped with neither the great depression nor pre-World War II, came. Here it was! Imagine if you can, a young American nurse who never saw a wringer washing machine. Suddenly, she is in Africa forty miles from her post office and gasoline, one hundred miles from staple foods, and without a telephone! She must provide water, lights, and heat for her residence and a clinic. She must do maintenance for all the above and transportation. Now add the one hundred to one thousand sick and well clients per day, plus deliveries and emergencies to attend at night. I reminded Jeanette that she would soon be in charge; she could make changes as we all did. I told her I had money for a new house in Saboba. Now, imagine if you can, a future committee stopping the building of a new Saboba house twice, but sending Jeanette to me with the complaints! It was not the intent of a previous clinic-friendly committee that, as matron, I should be responsible for housekeeping at both clinics. I was doing it at Nakpanduri for two MAPS nurses, but I had done it for twenty years! Jeanette went back to Saboba, but never seemed happy.

The New Mexico District News arrived. It contained a note from Mrs. Rowena Vanzant, WMs Director:

> It is hard to work around repairmen who are removing the fire damage in my office. Charlese has been busy training and/or placing new nurses for work in the

Ghana clinics. Pray for her; she has been battling illness and injuries since returning to Africa.

Only I knew just how much I needed prayer! For relaxation, I took my dog, Ebony, for a run down and then up the steep escarpment at 4 P.M. each afternoon. Children followed us and ran ahead with Ebony. Red-tailed, gray parrots flew above us and chattered down at us. When Ebony was small, the dog-faced baboons barked at us from the cliffs. Ebony ran to the car! I thought he might never be a protection, but eventually he challenged them.

♋ ♋ ♋

The Ghana Field Fellowship Annual Missionary Conference met in Accra on March 20–25. Carol and I drove to Accra. MAPS Nurse Diane had gone to help Jean Webster in Saboba, as Jeanette was ill in Tamale. A clinic committee report was presented by furlough-bound, Chairman Franklin McCorkle. The total patient visits to Nakpanduri Clinic that year was 26,258, with 2,964 antenatal visits, 438 post natal and newborn check-ups, with no maternal deaths or stillborn babies! That averaged over two thousand visits per month. There were five outpatient clinics per week in Nakpanduri. Monthly child welfare (well-baby) clinics were held in Bimbagu, Najong #2, Jimbari, Nasuan, and Sakogo on Tuesdays or Thursdays. There were two child welfare clinics per month, for Nakpanduri and nearby villages. Attendance at any outstation child welfare clinic might reach twelve hundred when giving seven hundred injections for childhood diseases or adult immunizations like cholera. We conducted 336 gospel services and one person or more nearly always came forward to accept Jesus as their personal Sacrifice.

Two resolutions had to do with clinics. Resolution #1: "The clinic Committee shall consist of . . . one nurse from each clinic and one Ghanaian member of Northern Ghana District Council." The reasoning was, "Their only two clin-

ics were in the north and Ghanaians knew there would be
no medical aid within their borders if they closed." Resolution #2: "Whereas, some clinics are staffed by nurses who
are not midwives as required by the Ghana Government,
and whereas, the only qualified midwife among the present nurses is Charlese Spencer, therefore be it resolved that
she be *Matron in Charge* of Assemblies of God maternity clinics until such time as both clinics are staffed with appointed
mission midwives."

Franklin McCorkle explained that the Clinic Committee
had already been using my credentials; this vote was just
to make it official. From the questions asked, I could tell
some considered it a power ploy by me, rather than, "saving the ranch!" "New king; new law!" I wanted to refuse on
the spot! However, I remembered my oft'-repeated prayer,
"Lord help me to do thy will and all you require of me." I did
not want the clinics to close. I knew what happened to the
people when clinics closed. I knew how hard it was on the
nurses to get them started again after they were closed even
temporarily. From questions asked and attitudes shown, I
knew opposition to clinics was a reality. The building of the
Saboba house for American nurses was in jeopardy again,
even though I had the money for the second time. The dirty,
precarious Saboba house might remain!

In early March, before the Missions Conference, I had
delivered a letter to Mr. Kwafu, Northern Administrative
Officer in Tamale. I told him we could not find cement for
construction. He wrote letters and got permission for us to
receive cement directly from the factory in Takoradi. Some
was allocated for contractors and for Northern Ghana on
certain days. After the conference in Accra, MAPS Nurse
Carol and I drove to Takoradi to the Ghana Cement Works.
I stopped a policeman to ask the way to the factory and
he exclaimed, "You're from Nakpanduri!" He was Bimoba
with the Ghana CID (CIA). He went to his station and asked
for time off. He directed us to the cement works. They said

Thursday, March 31 had been Northern Ghana day, but they had saved our five hundred bags. It cost over NC1500, one third of what it would have cost up north even if it were available! We learned that the manager, Mr. Moeller, and others at the cement works were Norwegians.

Carol had just visited family in Norway on her way to Ghana. They took us to a ship anchored in the Gulf of Guinea, where some lived with their family. I was introduced to Norwegian goat cheese and waffles; I'm still hooked! Mr. Moeller helped us find a lorry and driver. The Bimoba CID man found a policeman he knew to ride with our load to Nakpanduri. We were told that certain people were hijacking trucks, bribing the driver for more than we were paying him, and taking the load across borders to sell for more solid French Francs. You never saw your cement again. A Lebanese woman donated NC250 for transport. A building program in Ghana was no joke at that particular time, but we experienced miracles!

The Bimoba Area Easter Convention was held right in Nakpanduri. (Murphy's Law: Our load of cement arrived on Good Friday!) The fourteen Bimoba pastors had planned far ahead in their monthly meetings. The guest speaker was General Superintendent of Ghana Assemblies of God, E.J. Namyela-Panka. His wife, Karen, came with him; it was like a homecoming. They had pastored at Bunkpurugu many years before pastoring the Toma Church in Saboba. His job was now full-time; he pastored no more. The boarding school students were there on break; some came early because of the food shortage. The huge brush arbor was put beside the big Nakpanduri Church, built when nurses Joy King and Sharon Wallace were there. The Bimobas and I had received an announcement of Joy (King) Wheeler's wedding, so we knew Joy and Sharon would never be back in Ghana together. We were enjoying the fruits of their hard work, as those in Saboba area were enjoying what we built. Rev. Namyela-Panka was aware of all this! The people worshiped while exercising the gifts of the Holy Spirit. The pastors said they hoped to have groups of some size needing pastors when the present seven Bible school students returned to the area. John Saban Yajen and Thompson Tonlaar were in WAAST; Prince Masak, Daniel M., Thomas L., John J., and Daniel W. were in NGBI. A message came from Chief Nyankpen; he was a part of everything we did. He wanted to know if we were able to find certain food items. Even a chief was experiencing difficulty and he had money to pay. He signed, "May God bless you; we are praying for your foot."

In spite of much encouragement, I had surgery on my foot a third time and a finger on my right hand on April 15. I flew to Kumasi, had the surgery by the same doctor, and flew back to Tamale. The Driggers had gone on furlough. Jerry and Peggy Coburn were Kumasi resident missionaries. He helped me get parts sent up from Accra for brake repair on the Toyota. On April 17, I flew back to Tamale where MAPS Nurse Carol met me. We had the brakes repaired on the Toyota. She said the clutch on the Chevrolet pickup was going out again because of multiple drivers!

Among my many birthday cards was one from Mrs. Rowena Vanzant, WMS Director in New Mexico. Their District Council had just concluded. She updated me on activities like workweek at camp in Mountainair, Ministers' Seminar, youth and adult camps, girls' and women's retreats, and the USA General Council somewhere. James and Mary Lou Otts sent a card with a note from her:

> Last year we sent thirty dollars for two midwives in training. This year we are sending forty-five dollars to help three. As you know, James is a legislator in New Mexico. We were in Santa Fe almost three months early this year. Last Sunday we felt like strangers in our home church in Carlsbad.

Mary Lou, Vicki Otts, or Jeannie Mitchell usually sent the money to DFM. I had already been dividing it three ways.

Ruth Amos and Mary Zachary, both from Saboba, were in midwifery in Bolgatanga. Priscilla Panka was in nurse's training in Tamale; I was trying to get her into midwifery. She needed glasses as her head and eyes hurt when she studied. Our money was not for school fees; the young women were in government-supported schools. The matrons trained them as a favor to the mission. Our part was for extra books, a watch, an extra uniform, or travel at Christmas or school breaks. It was also to let the young people know we appreciated their desire to help in mission clinics. They would be released to the mission when they qualified. Mission policy was, "American nurses' budget must finance clinic." (In 2003, Teacher Samson Mankrom's third daughter, Sarah, phoned me from New Jersey, USA. She worked in a Ghana Bank. She reminded me that I had tried to get her into nursing or midwifery. I was serious about those indigenous clinics!)

Charles and Catherine Flach, the MAPS builders, were still busy at the coast. They wrote that they were building in the rains; they went where they were told. To know we were still on the building list was encouraging! Najong #1 pastor complained that they would soon be farming and they would not have a roof over their heads at church in the rainy season. I was trying to wait until the MAPS builder could carry some of the building responsibilities. For example, one Sunday, Big Red was stuck in a riverbed while going to Gbankoni with building supplies. We got there at noon when church had closed; they wanted another service! We dedicated a sack of cement and had a Jericho march around the church in anticipation of a bigger, better building! They had been making bricks for so long!

During the hunger months around March, April, and May, when the Bimobas' stored food was depleted and new crops were not yet producing, we gave food to seven hundred to one thousand people many days. The mothers would sometimes place their children under a tree and allow them to eat the dry cereal without cooking or dry milk without mixing it with water. They had come miles and were hungry; it broke my heart! Sometimes I felt I exaggerated when I said we fed more than seven hundred in attendance at child welfare clinics. Then MAPS Nurse Carol wrote in a form letter home:

> ...mothers lined up for malaria prophylaxis, vitamins, American surplus food, and to get their children weighed. If we weighed seven hundred toddlers, that put over one thousand mothers and children in one village to hear our messages. Some women received Christ into their life and that put families into churches.

In America, when I see a similar scenario on TV, where the children are so hungry, I am forced to look away, change channels, or cry. I wonder if Carol does!

One Friday, April 29, we made an emergency trip to the Baptist Hospital in Nalerigu. Willy Mae Berry, matron while Diane Lay was in Arizona on leave, told us that our new MAPS Nurse Holly had arrived in Tamale. They had methods of communication we did not. On Saturday, Carol and a Ghanaian drove to Tamale and brought Holly to Nakpanduri. She moved into our guest room, connected to our storeroom out behind our house. She and Carol agreed to share one of the two inside bedrooms when the MAPS builders arrived. MAPS Nurse Carol baked a cake and made a card with a lion and zebra on it for my birthday. Awuni, Peter, Jatuat, Emmanuel, Samson, Esther, Isaac, Holly, and Carol signed it. They gave it to me at a birthday party on Sunday, May 1; Tuesday would be a clinic day and too busy.

Jeanette wrote from Saboba, saying that the Ghanaian midwife I had gotten placed in Saboba was leaving. The clinics were registered as midwifery clinics, so it had been the intent of the clinic-friendly committee that I keep a midwife at Saboba when there was no American midwife there. Jeanette added, "Jean Webster is leaving on furlough; meet us in Tamale for a send-off." MAPS Nurse Holly and I drove the one hundred twenty miles to Tamale. We opened a bank account for her. She met Nurse Jeanette and MAPS Nurse Diane for the first time. We discussed the Saboba midwifery situation, but the Regional Matron had traveled to Accra. We were given an appointment for later. The McCorkles at Kumbungu were also due for furlough within days. We gathered at their house for a farewell party for all those leaving soon. Then we went to the airport to see Jean Webster off to America. I sent a note by her to MAPS builders Flachs in Takoradi. I told them about our guest room and offered Big Red for their move north. A reply came in a few days. They were expecting their freight via the Big River of the Black Star Line within a week. Their food and carpenter tools were on that ship. Finally, Mrs. Flach said, "The Hollingsworth family is going on furlough in July. They are loaning us their car while they are gone." Then 'my heart fell down, Paaa' as I read, "The new Chairman has not mentioned building a house for American nurses in Saboba, but perhaps he will!"

I wrote the new Chairman, "The building of a mission house for Saboba was approved along with Ghanaian nurses' quarters at both Saboba and Nakpanduri Clinics. Please, do we have permission for MAPS builder Flach to proceed with this as a project unit?" I discovered their decision in minutes mailed to me from a meeting to which I was not called. It was decided, so the minutes said, that the house could be built, but they would ask Bill Johnston to be the supervising missionary. That was fine with me! He lived in Yendi, a town closer to Saboba than Nakpanduri.

About mid-May, my foot was out of a bandage for the first time since leaving the USA last September. I had to travel a lot to find food, repair cars, or place midwives. The MAPS nurses were more confined to Nakpanduri. So, on a weekend we three went to Saboba. I wanted to see if they still had a midwife. MAPS Nurse Holly could see Saboba and meet the Konkombas. Janette and MAPS Nurse Diane had the house and clinic neat and organized. The midwife was still helping them. David Mankrom Nabegmado had graduated from Northern Ghana Bible Institute and was pastor of Turner Church, between the mission house and Saboba Market. He and I sat on the cement steps of the church and talked. He said, "I feel the Lord is telling me I will someday go to America." I knew it could happen; God got me to Africa that way. I said, "Obey God; if He wants you in America, He will also get you there." (Imagine, that wee orphan lad, born sixteen miles from the clinic and raised on American surplus powdered skim milk! He not only went to America, he went several times!)

We nurses went back to Nakpanduri in time for clinic on Monday. One morning I rushed Paul Jatuat Sillim, one of our clinic workers, to the Baptist Hospital in Nalerigu. Doctor Faile did an emergency appendectomy and said one more day might have been too late. While he was in surgery, I drove the short way to Gambaga and got our mail. Pastor Solomon K. Binambo from Saboba area wrote:

> Now I know nursing was not God's will for me. Madam, thank you for the Bible commentary. I was installed as pastor of Kokonzoli on May 14, and in June, we had our wedding there. I know your heart is with us and surely ours are with you.

Another letter was from Catherine Flach. She said the ship arrived with their food and carpenter tools. Her husband said to have people start cracking rock for gravel. What a hands-on gravel pit! That didn't sound like less work for me! She sent a list of items to buy like ceiling sheets, roofing, and plywood. She said she would be happy to take over the cooking because of the number of persons. Then a final note said:

> Addie has phoned. Polly has been in an accident on her way from Accra to teach at Southern Ghana Bible Institute in Saltpond. The vehicle was not badly damaged,

but Polly had some crushed vertebrae and will be in Tamale hospital at least six weeks.

Even with Paul Jatuat out recovering from surgery, I left the MAPS nurses to do clinic on June 8 and went to Tamale because of several serious situations. Number one was that the people in the Bimoba area were so hungry! The pickup was needed to haul American surplus food to villages, but the clutch was out. The correct clutch parts had arrived for Big Red! On my mini-furlough, a Chevrolet dealer in New Mexico sold me the wrong model part. A man coming out brought another. It was wrong! We wired Franklin McCorkle in Texas. He drove to Houston from Baytown and got the part. Later, the parts man phoned him, "I have sold you the wrong part." He had discovered a correction note at the bottom of a page! Not all WAWA (West Africa Wins Again) was in Africa! I almost wrote General Motors! Such a mess, hundreds of miles into the bush of Africa and trying to feed hungry people! The right clutch plate was put in! We needed fuels desperately by then. We could not haul food to the child welfare clinics without gasoline. I got the proper permit to fill a 45-gallon drum. There was a long line of lorries waiting with some drivers sleeping inside cabs. Some followed me to see if I had a proper permit; it was intimidating! They also hauled food for the people. I was medical for two tribes; if people died, they wouldn't need food. Which came first? The station attendant was nervous. I had the permit, so he gave me gasoline. On the way to Nakpanduri, I cried for the truckers, mothers, children, and Ghana!

I started buying building items on the MAPS builder's list. I found it had gone up three hundred percent since building the Pakinatiik church. While I was waiting for the clutch to be put in, I had visited Polly, the single lady who was in the Tamale hospital from the car accident. She said she had even prayed that I would come, for she knew I had back problems and was a mission nurse. I visited her a lot while the truck was being repaired. I also visited the Regional Matron about the midwife for Saboba. She wrote the person who threatened to remove the midwife, "You are not to withdraw any person at your own prerogative. The one sent to Saboba has not served six months, as stated in my original letter. If you have withdrawn the midwife from Saboba on the 7th of May, I instruct you to send her to Saboba indefinitely." The matron pledged to keep a midwife in Saboba until those we had in training could be assigned to the mission clinics!

Getting food and commodities like soap for the clinic became a crisis. Each time I requested food items at Gambaga, they had "already been assigned." I went to the Tamale Regional Offices. They advised me to write to the District Administrative Officer in Gambaga and ask to be a "Super Market Manager" for Nakpanduri area. Yes, as if I needed another job! I applied. Gambaga Council would receive that much more and it would not take away from those already receiving. I requested cases of soap, canned fish, sugar cubes, canned milk, and D batteries.

The next item required that I leave Big Red for the MAPS nurses and take the Toyota to Tamale. Big lorries left deep ruts; the muffler had been damaged and welded many times. It could no longer be welded and no new muffler was available in Tamale. I drove to Accra and had a new one put on. That was one thousand miles round trip. The heat in the north dries and cracks seals. Drive through the rain forest to Accra once or twice a year and you discover this! By the time I reached Accra, there was a puddle of water in the floorboard. I had the windshield re-sealed. The money for repairs came from New Mexico's DCAP (Youth Director), Eddie Lee. Rev. Osgood sent it on to me from mission headquarters. We were so blessed to have such help!

The heat in my spine, discovered before I left America for the shortened furlough, was increasing and going higher. I did not know whom I should inform, since those on the clinic committees were not "clinic-friendly." They might take the opportunity to send me home and close the clinics. When

Helen Kopp and I asked for a clinic committee in 1956, this was not what we had in mind! I knew officials did not want the MAPS builders to start clinic buildings or a house for American nurses in either Nakpanduri or Saboba until after a West African Conference in Ouagadougou, Upper Volta. Men would be there from mission headquarters in the USA! I had Ruby Johnson's leftover account because she wanted it to go for a new house for nurses in Saboba. I had thousands of dollars designated for that house from Clovis and other churches in New Mexico, Kansas, and West Texas; they wanted the nurses to have a new house! There is one saying I am famous for, "Money and power does funny things to people!" I gave it to God!

I wrote to my sister:

> At 4 A.M. I was delivering a baby. Then forty-five expectant mothers arrived for check-ups by me! MAPS Nurse Holly treated fifty people in general clinic. MAPS Nurse Carol went sixteen miles and found four hundred children plus mothers waiting at a child welfare clinic. We all had good Ghanaian help to interpret.
>
> At 2 P.M. we three left Nakpanduri on a buying trip to French Upper Volta. People in Ghana are about to revolt. We buy everything on the black market; hunt for it in homes. We line up to buy gasoline. Doctors are on strike; there is no diesel for lights in the hospitals. Tanks are controlling people in the streets of Tamale and Accra. The airports closed because of threats of arriving mercenaries. We hope to mail letters in Ouaga.

At one place, our lights flashed on an elephant. I turned the truck a bit and lit up a group of five. We arrived in Ouagadougou at 9 P.M., dead tired! The next day we drove up to a gasoline station and said, "Fill it up!" We ordered meat with a meal at a restaurant. The amazing thing was, I had seen all these things in Ghana in better times. However, planes were not flying out of Ouagadougou either because of possible mercenaries (paid soldiers) coming in to take advantage of civil unrest.

On the way back to Ghana, we saw elephants in daylight. One charged the Big Red Chevrolet. MAPS Nurse Holly yelled, "Faster, Charlese!" MAPS Nurse Carol got good pictures and said she dropped her camera lens-cover; I declined to return for it! Back in Nakpanduri Area, women were fighting for the last drop of water in pond or faucet. Teachers brought children to our clinic; they fainted. We fed them, gave them water and vitamins. Our hearts ached; we were frustrated. I wrote the Regional Administrative Officer to find food and we'd haul it to the people! As far away as the Toronto Star reported, "The people in Ghana have planted five times and rain did not come. The Baptist Medical Center said they were receiving about ten severely under-nourished children daily and should admit twice that number!" A chief said, "We will get through; we do not die of starvation, but while we are weak, a disease kills us." In Lome, Togo, Joseph Mills, editor of the student paper called *WAAST Outlook* commented:

> The Ghana Government declared a national week of repentance and prayer. Righteousness makes a nation great; sin is a disgrace to any nation. Proverbs 14:34.

A letter from a WAAST Student read:

> I am writing three research papers at one time! I ordered some books; I paid for only a part of them so I could buy soap. Madam, things in Togo and Ghana are so costly. I am telling the truth; I bought no luxury item! Yours faithfully, John S. Yajen.

We sent dollars to Reverend Jackson for help to our students.

One clinic helper, Paul Jatuat Sillim, was accepted into the School of Nursing in Bawku Hospital, just forty miles north.

I dreaded the day he was to start, but in all fairness, we must let him advance. Our list of Ghanaian nursing and midwifery students for mission clinics was impressive. We would need housing for them at our clinics. The MAPS builders, Charles and Catherine Flach, did arrive in Nakpanduri on August 31, 1977. She took over the kitchen with Emmanuel, our regular house helper. They cooked pancakes and sent to workers who might not eat otherwise! Ghanaian pastors, clinic, and building workers saw the Flachs working so hard, they all tried to keep up! I was making sure river sand, water, cement, lumber, nails, metal roofing sheets, window frames, louvers, and workers were available when Builder Flach needed them, especially items in the metric system. One of Mr. Flach's workers was a Dagomba (by tribe) called, "Big Man." I admired his ability then and met him later when my opinion was again confirmed! I kept books for each building project, money in my account at mission headquarters and my personal account in New Mexico. My niece Roxanne wrote:

> Dan is building us a house a mile away; we will move January 1978. Erin Michelle is proudly dressing herself and Hannah Marie is walking. Your house payment is eighty-eight dollars per month.

Years later, when I moved into my house, the payment was over four hundred dollars because of taxes and insurance.

In early September, a letter came from former MAPS Nurse Claudia. She wrote, "Dear *Ethel*, I received your form letter telling about the four new nurses." At times, young nurses voiced their feelings about the lack of clothing worn by clinic clients; I remembered when they wore less! I also remember the nude streakers in American colleges! To concerned MAPS nurses, I would say, "Don't look, Ethel!" Claudia started calling me Ethel. "Can I come for a visit in October? If it is to be, *den God dey*!" (Then God is there.)"

The West African Conference convened in Ouagadougou, Upper Volta (now Burkina Faso), September 7-11, 1977.
Ten Bimoba Pastors, two MAPS nurses, and I went in the Big
Red Chevrolet from Ghana. They all wanted to see elephants;
we saw none. Two top officials from the USA, Philip Hogan
and Morris Williams, came from our World Headquarters
in Missouri. Don Corbin, assistant to Morris Williams, came
from Abidjan, Ivory Coast. Ghana Mission Chairman came
with the news that Jeanette Boteler wanted to leave Saboba
Clinic. That was a blow! In all fairness, Saboba was so run
down! It needed a Ruby Johnson or a Charlese Spencer to
make "all systems go!" My heart cried when I thought of
how beautiful it once was. Whoever was there, it needed a
new house! After an official meeting, it was decided that,
"Saboba Clinic would close November 1977; Jeanette and
MAPS Nurse Diane could both go home now. Nakpanduri
Clinic would close in January 1978 when it was time for
MAPS Nurse Carol to leave. MAPS Nurse Holly would leave
a bit early. It sounded workable. However, when the officials
of the Ghana Churches were told, they were not willing for
the clinics to close and leave two tribes without medical aid.
They were concerned that if the mission had no service to
the Ghanaian people, their visas may not be renewed. As for
me, the heat and pain in the spinal area made me willing to
return to the USA; I left with the other nurses.

As surely as I knew I was to go to Africa, I knew it was
time to return permanently to the USA. It had been a full
and rewarding life. I thank God for a mission organization
with all departments that allows one to fulfill a calling. I am
grateful to God for the overwhelming love and support of
my home District Council of New Mexico and for Kansas
District Council that adopted me when I taught nursing in
that state. West Texas District supplied two coworkers and
helped support the clinics. Finally, I am thankful for the support of my family, friends, nurse and midwifery coworkers,

MAPS (nurses, builders, and others), and interested donors. God reward you; I cannot.

I am reminded again of the impression I had at age twenty, "Get up and go to SBI (SAGU), I've got *something* I want you to do."

1. In Africa, when we saved lives from snakebite or tended a mother and child at the hour of birth, I said, "Ah so this is that something God wanted me to do!"

2. When we helped in two medical field-tests, one a sulfonamide, for control and cure of leprosy and one to eradicate yaws with penicillin, I said, "Ah, so this is that something God wanted me to do!"

3. When we gave the good news message to one more person, another family, or at head man's or chief's compound that they did not have to supply the blood, from chicken or animal, for a sacrifice, because God had already supplied it for them through His Son, and they believed and we watched them grow into spiritual maturity, I said, "Ah, so this is that something God wanted me to do!"

4. When each church or clinic building we helped to build was dedicated, I said, "Ah, so this is that something God wanted me to do!"

5. When I helped to rescue two girls, in different tribes, literally setting the young generation free from slavery (being promised at birth and body mutilation) so they could go to school or choose whom to marry, I said, "Ah, so this is that something God wanted me to do!"

6. When I receive letters from young people telling what they are doing with the education I had some small part in, I say, "Ah, so this is that something God wanted me to do!"

7. When I spoke in U.S. churches and saw young people dedicate themselves to specific needs of their generation, I said, "Ah, so this is that something God wanted me to do!"

To be sure I did that something He wanted me to do, I did it all to the best of my ability.

Epilogue

Nursing Education and Retirement
Nostalgic Visit to Ghana, West Africa

AFTER RESTING FOR ONE year, I started teaching obstetrics in the University of Albuquerque; it was my original diploma program turned junior collage ADN program. After one year, the director decided I should use my Masters Degree to save the Ladder Nursing Program she had started at Luna Vo-Tec and Highland University in Las Vegas, New Mexico. I hesitated to leave my home in Albuquerque again, but did. In three years, I graduated three classes of practical nurses at Luna Vo-Tec and three classes of RN's at Highland University in Las Vegas. By then, I had advanced from cane to crutches and visited Lovelace Clinic in Albuquerque, where my records were kept. I was diagnosed "Arachanoiditis." Using the computer at the UNM Library, I researched the condition and it was confirmed: Chronic sterile meningitis; no treatment, no cure, will advance. I now get around by using a motorized wheelchair. The pain from inside the spine to the nerve endings on the skin cannot be described. Any individual cases I've known are now deceased.

209

My neuromuscular medical records have always been at Lovelace Medical Center in Albuquerque. In 1983 I went into Lovelace Hospital to see if the condition could be helped. I was still on the ministerial list in NMDC, so they visited me.Pastor R. K. George, my pastor at First Family Church, was also Assistant District Superintendent of NMDC. When he visited me in the hospital, he would always say, "When you get better, First Family Church is going to send you back to Ghana for a visit . . ." I hoped, but never believed it would happen. There was no medical help available except pain control, so I resigned my job and moved to my house in Albuquerque.

In May 1987, Pastors R. Kenneth George and LaVerne Elder, my Aunt Leonora Wister and I flew via TWA to New York's Kennedy Airport and to Heathrow Airport in London. Two of our suitcases were missing already. By taxi, we crossed London to Gatwick Airport to fly British Caledonia Airline to Lagos, Nigeria. We paged and tried to phone Nurse Tadimie Jagir, from Saboba, who was working in Nigeria, but failed to reach him. Ghanaians who met us at the Accra Airport were Reverends N. Panka, S. Asore, D. Nabegmado, Big man Allasan, MAPS Builder Flach's helper, and Peter, Mata's brother. Mata was the wife of Abraham, our Saboba yardman when Ann Fisher and I were at Saboba. We met the Goodwin and Bowman missionary families. John and Amonna Sue Goodwin and their three daughters, Karen, Cherisse, and Laneice, had invited us to Ghana. The next morning we visited the Ghana General Council offices and printing press. Reverend Namyela-Panka and his wife, Karen, lived in quarters above those offices with their two youngest sons. Two of their daughters, Priscilla and Blondina, came to greet us.

John Goodwin chauffeured us on a tour of Ghana in one of the four Range Rovers supplied by Reverend Jimmy Swaggart for two ambulances and two business managers of the clinics. On our second day in Ghana, John Goodwin, Kenneth George, LaVerne Elder, and Aunt Leonora left Accra. They drove from Accra, through Kumasi and the Ashanti Forest (jungle). They stopped to greet the chief of Techamentia, a village where Helen and I set up a clinic in 1955. Leonora was introduced to the Chief as my *aunt who was age 80 and still had her own teeth*; he was highly amused! John drove the group on to NGBC at Kumbungu in the north of Ghana, where I was to meet them. I flew by Ghana Airways to Tamale Airport. Reverends Solomon Ayaba, Northern Ghana District Superintendent, drove from Tamale to meet me, and Peter Yamusah, Principal of NGBI, came from Kumbungu. They told me that the Bunkpurugu chief had died.

I had sent a letter with forms for certain ones to complete to help me write my book. They said that when one form was for Chief Nyankpen about the 1959 incident at Najong #2, they paid lorry-fare for a man to rush it to him. They said if he got the letter, it might lift his heart and he might improve. The man arrived, only to learn the chief had died. It put me on a massive guilt-trip that I had left Bimobaland without personally bidding him farewell! You do not do that to a friend, even less to a chief! I was so ill and so destroyed in 1978! I rode to NGBC at Kumbungu with Peter Yamusah, as I was to meet John and the land travelers there.

Within hours, the weary, dusty Range Rover travelers arrived and my Aunt Leonora declared the trip *unforgettable!* Staying in Kumbungu stirred mixed emotions. I was so glad to be there, but we slept in a new *guesthouse* and a generator produced electricity until about 9:00 P.M. Both could have been made possible by my leaving. They had asked to borrow one of the two generators I had purchased in London. I had not built the house in Saboba for American nurses; the money went somewhere. My kerosene chest freezer was in the room where we travelers ate our meals. Simon Jato Masak from Najong #2 was teaching there. His wife, Eunice, had gone to visit her family in Najong #1; the girl we once rescued was her sister. Simon Jato's father was the headman who held my car keys so those of us being beaten could not escape on that August day in 1959.

Emmanuel Billin, a student, was my cook in Nakpanduri for four years. He did not have money to support his wife and daughter, Hannah and Paulina, at the school. Paulina was in primary school; they still had only the one miracle. He begged me to return to Ghana and help them have another child; that involved time!

The next morning, after only one night at NGBC, formerly NGBI, we drove north. We stopped at the Baptist hospital in Nalerigu and ate a meal with nurses Diana and Willie Mae. They gave the group, all except me, a tour of the hospital as my aunt was a Baptist member in Phoenix and knew Diana Lay. As we entered the edge of Nakpanduri, the people started calling, "Welcome Madam." At the clinic, we met Paul Jatuat Sillim, David Kansuk Laar, and Midwife Mary Samson, another sister to Eunice Masak. They were free to choose their occupation and lifetime mates. The clinic had gone somewhat indigenous. John Goodwin and a Ghanaian business manager were managing Nakpanduri and Saboba clinics from Accra.

Pastor Jeremiah Kombat was still at the local church. We learned that his wife, Mahatabel, had recently been killed in a lorry accident! Memories of their posh wedding ran by me. On Sunday, May 24, the morning service seemed to be dedicated to survivors of the Najong #2 incident. Those injured were called out and honored. The beloved deacon from Najong #2, Elijah Kombat, was there. I was extremely sad that Lay-pastor Samson, the father of the girl we rescued, had died. Instead, his wife, the mother of Eunice and Mary, was there to be honored. As I had been told, Chief Nyankpen Libagitib from Bunkpurugu had died, and I did not see his wife, Waniib, there. I was asked to give greetings. As I looked over the congregation, I could remember incidents about almost all in the packed pews. A youth choir sang and some stepped out to speak about the fact that they were free to pursue the occupation of their choice because of the effects of the Najong #2 incident. Reverend George was guest speaker. The pastors and people said he preached like he was reading their faces (minds). The pastors presented him with a Ghanaian smock. He was not too comfortable with that term for a shirt!

At an afternoon banquet, Presbyter John Saban Yajen read a paper he had prepared; Reverend George gave me a copy. It read:

> Proclamation concerning Charlese Spencer, to R. Kenneth George at Nakpanduri, Ghana, West Africa. Guests of honor, ministers, invited guests, ladies and gentlemen! I express my gratitude for seeing Miss Charlese Spencer in Bimobaland again. Let us say a big hallelujah to God for blessing and guiding her during her successful ministry in Ghana and especially in the Bimoba communities. We Bimobas were hidden from the good news of Jesus. In the 1950s, because of God-fearing people like this lady, our people first met the Gospel. As we know, laying a foundation is always the greatest task. This lady met hardships, even to the verge of death, but since it was the will of God that Bimobas also should be saved, she was victorious. The event of August 20, 1959 still roams within us as a day of both sorrow and victory. A Christian girl was betrothed to a man who suspected the girl would not agree to marry him. He put her into Kwont to brainwash her into marrying him. Pastors, elders of the churches, some peace officers and Miss Spencer were beaten mercilessly when they went to remove her from her captors. Miss Spencer went to USA for rest. We hardly thought she would return, but when she recovered, she joyfully returned to us. She sacrificed her life to bring us the light; it has yielded grain; may God bless her! Miss Spencer is also remembered for building churches at Jelik, Pakinatiik, Sisi, Gbankoni, Bombil, the Nakpanduri parsonage and nurses' quar-

ters at the Bimoba clinic. These still exist although she left us suddenly. This lady also equipped the pastors by teaching area seminars and getting scholarships for pastors and student for further education beyond what Bimobaland had to offer. I, John Saban, am one given such a chance. Let us be thankful to God for giving us this competent, devoted, charismatic leader. Through her and her colleagues Bimobaland was converted to Christianity. Miss Spencer is in our midst today. Probably she said, `I will go back one more time to my people, the Bimobas, before I die.' There are many things left undone in Bimobaland. We appeal to you that you come back once more to our saddened Bimobaland and serve in the Master's vineyard. Paul said, `For me to live is Christ and to die is gain.' Miss Spencer, Bimobas, especially the Christians, will continue to have your name on their lips.

Signed, Rev. John Saban Yajen,
Nakpanduri Section Presbyter.

(It was John Saban's father who gave the command both to kidnap the girl and to beat her rescuers.) Reverend John Kombat, a senior pastor in the area, sang a special song at the banquet. He was among those honored, as he was also beaten. He led us to sing that same song on our way to the police station in 1959. The words were, "My Lord is able— He's able to set the captive free." The banquet of rice and hot pepper meat sauce was a huge success!

My Aunt Leonora had become violently ill and we left her with the watchman, Lari, while we went to church. She said he stayed with her every minute. We treated her for malaria and dehydration with meds and salts John carried. When she was almost comatose, I sat on her bed to spoon-feed her Jell-O and hydrating salt water. I had assigned mothers to do this for their babies at the clinics; now it was my duty.

On Monday morning, while I stayed to care for my auntie, the others drove 40 miles to Bawku, Tili, and back. An anniversary of the Tili Naba's death was being celebrated; he was a Christian. John Goodwin's brother, Sydney, was buried in Bawku after being severely burned by an accident at Tili. Reverend and Mrs. George were friends of Sydney and his wife, Sandra, and their one child, Gwenda. (Thelma, Mrs. Homer Goodwin, reminded me that the Paul Weidmans also have a son, younger than Sydney, buried in West Africa.)

While the visitors were gone to Bawku, area pastors, including John Yajen, Joseph Kombat and James Lambon, came to sit with me on the front verandah of the rock bungalow. They insisted on knowing the details of why I left so abruptly in 1978; I had not told them. Some of them had been discriminated against for taking up for me in my absence. They also told me of persecution coming upon the Christian church. Already some of their houses had been ransacked and burned; they felt their lives were in danger. The situation fully exploded in 1994. John, who wrote so many times of his fears of being beheaded was actually beheaded for his faith in 1994. A Member of Parliment, visiting me in America in 1997, told me what happened to him.

Those who traveled to Bawku returned about noon. We spent some time in prayer at the clinic with Paul Jatuat, David K. Laar, Awuni Dubik, Midwife Mary Samson, and others. Some children followed us everywhere to tease, especially one lad rolling an old lorry tire. As late as it was, we drove down the Gushiago moto'way toward Yendi. Near Savalugu we bent back sharply and turned east at Wapuli where Reverend Emmanuel Gondow Wumbei was pastor. (In 1994, Pastor Emmanuel walked and hitchhiked 400 miles to Accra to send me a letter telling me what was happening to the Christians. He died soon after that. He had once told me, when you get so hungry, then sickness can kill you." I believe that he died of starvation. That makes my heart pain.) It was dark when we got to Saboba. Peter Brahma, the

Fulani pastor at Toma Church and the Turner Church Pastor and members had been waiting for hours.

We set up camp inside the old Saboba house. Money I had raised for the second time had obviously NOT gone for a new house for the nurses in Saboba. John Goodwin and I took Reverend George to see if he wanted to stay, for privacy, in Ruby's add-on bedroom the NMDC had helped to finance. We stooped to avoid drooping ceiling sheets with hanging cobwebs mixed with lizard droppings. Pastor George quickly declined and went to put his cot up in the middle of the front room. John Goodwin put up his cot beside that one and we three women migrated to the one bedroom in the main house. When we went to brush our teeth, we discovered that the watchman in Nakpanduri, thinking he was doing us a favor, had put only hot tea with milk and sugar in one of our two thermos jugs. They were a gallon size, but we had emptied one with water on the journey to Saboba. The tea was sour and dank; we could not even brush our teeth with it.

Next morning, the two Saboba congregations, Turner and Toma, joined for a celebration at Toma with Pastor Brahma Fulani as MC. The people wanted news about every past Saboba clinic nurse. Again, I could remember incidents about almost every person present. I had delivered many of them at the clinic. My happiness made me oblivious to the mid-day heat under a metal roof with no ceiling. Once, during preliminaries, music, testimonies, presentations and my greetings, I noticed Ken George elbow John Goodwin. I heard him say, "If this goes on another hour, they've lost me!" After that, he received a gift of another N.T.'s smock and was the main speaker! Some circuit pastors like Abarika and Dondow had footed it for 40 miles. When Leonora asked if they were not afraid of snakes, they replied, "No, we just walked and sang; we were going to see Madam." What a humbling experience; I cried a lot! After the service, families lined up to show me their children or tell me what their adult children were doing. The nurse was there who ended his letters, "Oh, when will we meet and laugh again?" Sure enough, we were *meeting and laughing again!*

John Goodwin came back from the air-conditioned Range Rover, to which the other travelers had retired. He reached over the crowd, took my hand while he explained that we had a schedule to keep. We drove up to the mission house where a banquet of rice, meat, and seasonings was waiting out on the palaver porch toward the market. My Aunt Leonora re-named it *Solomon's porch.* Perhaps the major cook in Saboba, Amos Biyimba, had something to do with the cooking. The women served. Helen Beso Magbaan, now employed at the clinic, served Leonora and me. Leonora said she thought Helen was one of the most beautiful women she had ever seen. Her husband, David B. Magbaan was there, but he did not look well.

As we ate, pastors talked about memories. Reverend Emmanuel Gondow read a scripture that I had used on one of my partings from Saboba. He said I ended by saying, "If you want your people to be strong, feed them the Word of God!" He showed us where he had written it in his Bible. One pastor asked, "Do you know how Madam Spencer taught us who worked in the house or clinic to pay tithes? When the moon died (at the end of the month), she gave us two envelopes. One had our money; the other had God's money that we were told to put in the church offering the next Sunday!" They paid their pastor's salary that way!

The food, as usual, was quite zesty with pepper and we still had no water to drink since the day before. Oh yes, there was water, but it was not even offered to us since they knew how we treated the water we drank. Our suitcases had never caught up with us; we could not change clothing. When we were out of the Range Rover our clothing was wet; inside the cooled vehicle it became stiff like cardboard. I sent word to Jagir, Tadimi's father, to come the short way from chief's village of Kpatapaab. Chief Quadin had died and his son was chief. Of course, Jagir was still anxious to know about his son who was a nurse and had gone, not to just to a school of nursing in Tamale, but to Nigeria. I told him we tried to find him in Lagos, but did not.

We drove 40 miles to Yendi, where we found bottled coca-colas, cooled only in a tub of water. They were delicious and wet. They revived us enough to drive on to Kumbungu where Reverend George spoke in chapel at NGBC. He was given another Northern Ghana smock, presented by Emmanuel Nantogma, a teacher who eventually came to America for a higher degree at Fuller Theological Seminary in California. The Range Rover left to go back to the coast by way of the Volta Region. Reverend Peter Yamusah had made reservations for Aunt Leonora and me to fly via Ghana Airways back to Accra the next morning. Big Man Allasan met us at Accra airport. The pain in my back had gradually increased with a vengeance on that trip; I was glad to fly. Ghana Airways had found our luggage (two bags) lost by TWA and missing since London. Mail from Amonna Sue McCorkle Goodwin's family was inside one! Among other visitors who came to our quarters to greet us after we got back from the north were the Pankas, the Asores, the Nabegmados, and the Obangs who were installed as pastors in Central Assembly on our last Sunday in Accra. Our traveling group, except me, made a visit to Southern Ghana Bible College and the coastal slave trade castle at Elmina. I knew I should not travel again until the long journey to America.

That evening, Joseph Mills, SGBC Principal who once visited TorC, New Mexico, Adeline Wichman, and Pauline Smith, long-time missionaries, came from Saltpond. We all ate the evening meal with John and Amonna Sue's family. On the last day, Rev. and Mrs. Bowman took us out to eat at the Golden Dragon for Chinese food before we left Ghana.

༄ ༄ ༄

Saboba Clinic is now Saboba Medical Center with a Doctor Jean and her Med. Tech. husband, Robert. They have a phone and two-way radio; they have electricity from the Volta River Dam Project and piped-in water. They spent New Year's with me once and said, they just had to meet "Madam" who prayed for a doctor and said, "I am just better than nothing." Dr. Jean said, "I am that doctor; God was in process of answering your prayers."

What more could I ask than to see the results of my labor at the relatively young age of 59. That is the age at which I was forced to retire.

NOSTALGIC RETURN TO GHANA, 1987: 1. D. & D. Sierra taxied us to TWA. 2-3. On the plane. 4-6. Goodwins who planned and drove vehicle in Ghana, Chairman Bowman who invited us, Ghanaians who met and greeted us. 7-9. David M-N and my mom in USA, his wife, Comfort, with my aunt in Accra and their daughters in dresses from Karen H. 10-12. First Family visitors and Ghana officials. 13. NGBI in Kumbungu where officials got their start and we visitors met in N. Ghana.

About the Author

PERHAPS ONLY AN UNMARRIED person could have time for a degree, license, diploma or certificate in technology, banking, medicine, clergy and education involving eleven institutions of learning above the four-year high school level. I have lived, gone to school, or practiced these professions on three continents. This produced friends only defined by mass, horde, throng, or multitude; that alone could trigger a few enemies! Forced retirement at age 59, caused by a diagnosis of Arachanoiditis (neuro-muscular deterioration), was the greatest physical blow I ever endured. It advanced from crutches to the present motorized wheelchair for pain control. Since I am the one with the pain, I can tell you, "It is *not* controlled!" However, I'm grateful for the medical assistance and prayers on my behalf!

Printed in the United States
47438LVS00005B/13-36